Baking
Artisan Bread

WITH NATURAL STARTERS

Andrews McMeel Publishing
a division of Andrews McMeel Universal
1130 Walnut Street, Kansas City, Missouri 64106

www.andrewsmcmeel.com

www.farmtomarketbread.com

18 19 20 21 22 RR2 10 9 8 7 6 5 4 3 2 1

ISBN: 978-1-4494-8784-3

Library of Congress Control Number: 2018944527

ATTENTION: SCHOOLS AND BUSINESSES

Andrews McMeel books are available at quantity discounts with bulk purchase for educational, business, or sales promotional use. For information, please e-mail the Andrews McMeel Publishing Special Sales Department: specialsales@amuniversal.com.

Baking
Artisan Bread
WITH NATURAL STARTERS

MARK FRIEND

Photography by
THOMAS GIBSON

Andrews McMeel
PUBLISHING®

CONTENTS

PREFACE

My journey with bread started by accident. I grew up behind a doughnut shop in Dallas, Texas. When an opportunity came along for me to be employed there at age fourteen, I jumped at it. The doughnut shop allowed me to make money, which meant independence. I was proud of my ability to go to work at 4 a.m., but whenever I did oversleep, the other baker would come knock on my window to wake me up. Working in that doughnut shop through high school led to more jobs in bakeries during college. I learned something new from every place I worked. I was intrigued by the art and science of baking and driven by the desire to make the best-quality bread I could.

Although I pursued other avenues of knowledge—psychology and nursing—bread kept calling me back. It was a craft in which I had experience, and I became convinced that I would never be without work if I pursued bread baking.

After it became clear that baking would be my career, I did not realize how much more I needed to learn. There was a lot of trial and error along the way. I learned the ins and outs of traditional and "modern" bread baking from working in small French bakeries and small wholesale bakeries. Yet the time I spent in my own home kitchen was just as important and just as full of lessons toward refining my craft. Finally, in 1986, early in the growing interest across the country in artisan bread, I decided to focus on naturally leavened breads. I am drawn to artisan bread baking because it is a return to the true craft of baking. Artisan bread returns to techniques used prior to production methods introduced during the industrial revolution. My purpose as an artisan baker is to bake the best bread I can.

I was approached by a group of investors who wanted to start a San Francisco sourdough bakery and needed a production manager. I accepted, and they sent me to San Francisco to train with Claudio Cantore, a third-generation Italian baker. I learned the secrets of the sourdough process from Claudio, and he is still a mentor to me today. Over the next seven years, I honed my sourdough skills at Pacific Baking Co. in Kansas City, Kansas.

I wanted the ability to control all the decisions affecting the quality of the bread I was making, so in 1993 I left Pacific Baking Co. to start Farm to Market Bread Company with Fred Spompinato. Fred was a good friend and fellow baker at Pacific Baking Co. Fred would later leave Farm to Market to start Fervere Artisan Bakery in Kansas City, Missouri. We invested $10,000 of our own money and took out a $10,000 loan to purchase an oven and a small mixer. We set up in the back of a café and traded bread for rent. Farm to Market Bread was dedicated to making everything the way bread was originally made. We used natural starters and hand-formed the loaves. And we baked the loaves using time-honored methods like hand forming, use of natural starters, natural ingredients, long fermentation, and hearth baking. Everything we did was with the goal of making true artisan bread.

As Farm to Market grew, we had to explore the possibility of using other automated equipment to meet the demand for our bread. We always maintained the basic ingredients of flour, water, starter, and salt, as well as the expertise from centuries of artisan bakers. With every decision we made as we expanded, quality always came first.

Today, twenty-five years later, Farm to Market Bread is still committed to making bread the natural way.

Part of a baker's commitment is to pass knowledge along, and that's why I'm writing this book. I have been fortunate to learn from many master bakers, including Claudio Cantore, Professor Raymond Calvel, Michel Suas, Lionel Vatinet, and Thom Leonard. They have been so generous with their time and expertise that I feel I need to do that, too. It's all part of the love of great bread.

Once you have made your own starter and baked that first loaf, you'll be hooked. You'll appreciate the baker's art even more. You'll visit an artisan bakery and see things with new eyes once you know how sourdough goes from starter to loaf and what it takes to create the perfect artisan baking environment.

I want you to be able to make and eat great bread from your own kitchen, as well as from Farm to Market.

MARK FRIEND

INTRODUCTION

The best way to appreciate artisan bread is to get in the kitchen and make it yourself, step by step. Naturally fermenting a starter, mixing it with flour to form a dough, mixing the dough to add structure, letting the dough slowly rise, forming the loaf, and then baking it are techniques that date back 7,000 years. Today, amid a return to the artisan way of baking, we continue that history of bread as we bake in our own kitchens, walking in the footsteps of the thousands of bakers who have gone before us.

In the following pages, you will learn that two of the most important components of true artisan bread baking are a healthy starter and attention to detail. You will develop your baker's intuition and grow in your ability to "know the dough," like so many bakers before us did, so that extra water or flour can be added just because you "know."

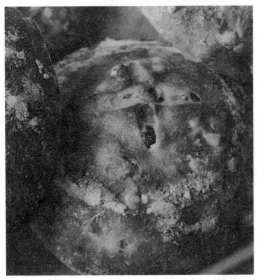

We start with the starters, which are pre-ferments, from the well-known San Francisco Sourdough Starter (page 26), which gives that distinctive tang to bread; to the French Levain (page 31), which is less dense and sour; to the Rye Starter (page 37), which brings a richness to rye bread; and in a later chapter the Italian pre-ferment known as Biga (page 116). Biga is not a starter, but rather a pre-ferment made with baker's yeast and fermented for 12 to 16 hours prior to the final dough, creating a nutty flavor.

Some of the baker's terms you encounter in this book may differ from those that you are familiar with. For example, we use proof sometimes instead of rise. Proof came from bakers seeing the dough rise as proof that the yeast of the starter was working. Essentially, they mean the same thing.

Start your bread journey in this book with the San Francisco Sourdough Starter (page 26) and, specifically, the San Francisco Sourdough Boule (page 58). This loaf will let you practice the art of artisan bread, from weighing the ingredients to mixing the dough, letting the dough ferment, forming the loaves and letting them proof, and baking like an artisan baker. And all with delicious results.

There are, admittedly, a lot of steps to follow in the tradition of artisan bread baking. All these techniques have been created and passed down through generations of bakers. As you learn about the importance of starters in bread baking, you will progress toward making the perfect loaf simply by knowing and responding to exactly what that bread dough needs. And I will help you every step of the way.

CHAPTER ONE

WHAT YOU NEED
TO GET STARTED

WE ALL KNOW THAT TOOLS ARE IMPORTANT to building something or accomplishing a task, whether it's playing a symphony or fixing a light switch. It's no different when it comes to bread. Good tools help make the recipe easier to produce and enhance your chances of creating a good loaf of bread.

Before we bake our first loaf, let's look at the tools that will make this process more successful. These are the tools that make the mechanics of bread baking easier and that the bakers at Farm to Market find helpful.

THE ARTISAN BREAD BAKER'S TOOLBOX

The right tool or piece of equipment will make the process more efficient. You may already have a fine alternative for some of these in your kitchen, so use the tools that will get the job done, and done well.

- 5-quart (4.7 liter) stainless-steel bowl
- Electric stand mixer (optional)
- Work surface
- Baking stone
- Gram scale
- 2 proof baskets, 8 ½ inches (21 cm) in diameter by 3 inches (7.6 cm) in height
- Oven peel
- Food thermometer
- Bread lame or razor blade
- Cooling rack
- Serrated knife
- Metal and plastic scrapers

A 5-quart (4.7 liter) stainless-steel bowl with a diameter of 13 inches (33 cm) and height of 4 ½ inches (11.5 cm) will accommodate dough yielding two loaves. Stainless steel is a good choice not only for mixing, but also for making cleanup easier, particularly if the dough is sticky. Do not plan to use the bowl from your stand mixer for mixing by hand; it is shaped to fit the attachments, not your hands. Also, the bowl from your mixer is simply not wide enough to be used for cloche baking (see page 54), in which you invert the bowl over a loaf to let it steam-bake.

You may already have a large pottery bowl, perhaps a family heirloom. While this type of bowl can be used for mixing your dough by hand, it will also not work well for cloche baking.

You can make great bread by hand—and some of the best bread is made by hand—but you can also use a **stand mixer** for mixing, if you prefer. Using an electric stand mixer allows you to vary your approach to developing the dough, as well as saving time and energy.

The KitchenAid Classic stand mixer is easy to clean, and its 325 watts of power are enough to adequately mix the dough. Throughout this book, the recipes will provide mixing times for both hand and electric stand mixing. Other brands are fine, but just be sure that the mixer includes a spiral dough hook.

A **work surface** for mixing and even proofing can be easily cleaned with a metal scraper. Oftentimes the work surface is the kitchen table or counter, but if you want a dedicated area for bread baking (or your kitchen is not large), consider purchasing a hardwood board, measuring about 18 by 24 inches (45 by 60 cm) from a restaurant supply store, kitchen shop, or hardware store.

Baking stones are important in making artisan bread. Heating a stone to high temperatures for baking is one of the best ways a home baker can achieve the crust and crumb of true artisan bread. The stones are usually circular or rectangular, but the most important thing is that you have one that fits in your oven. You can find them at big-box stores, kitchen shops, or online. One of the best stones we have found is available from Pampered Chef. You place the stone in the oven, on the rack on which the bread will be baked, and preheat the stone in the oven while your dough proofs. Baking stones can be stored in your oven except during the self-cleaning cycle.

The **gram scale** is used to measure flour, water, and salt, as well as any other ingredients. We use it for accuracy. And because accuracy is important, we prefer using the metric system to weigh the ingredients in grams. However, we also include volume measurements with the recipes in this book.

You might want to initially dismiss this measuring method as being too much trouble, but first try a little test. Fill three identical cups with flour. Now measure each of these on a gram scale and note the differences in each one. You will be amazed. No doubt about it, using a gram scale produces a more accurate measure. Gram scales priced from $20 to $30 are great for home use, and are available at Bed Bath & Beyond, as well as kitchen shops and better grocery stores.

Proof baskets help the loaves keep their shape through proofing, and are usually used for the final proof of levain and rye doughs. If this stage is done in a solid bowl of any kind, the bread will stick and lose its shape when transferred to an oven peel. The proof basket should be a wicker basket lined with linen.

Prepare the proof basket by coating the linen with flour and tapping out the excess. When you are ready to put the dough into the proof basket, place the top of the loaf on the bottom of the basket so the underside of the loaf is visible. This way, when you invert the basket onto the oven peel, the top will be facing up and ready for the oven. The basket will support the dough as it proofs, preventing the loaf from losing its shape.

A good source for proofing baskets is the San Francisco Baking Institute. Not only do they have a variety of affordable baskets, but the proceeds from the baskets go to scholarship funds for students attending the school.

An **oven peel** is a paddle-like tool used by bakers to slide loaves of bread into and out of the oven. Although you can find them made of sheet metal or aluminum, wood is recommended because it releases the formed loaf more easily onto the baking stone in the oven. Peels come in many sizes, so be sure to pick one that has a handle about 15 inches (38 cm) in length. This is a good length for most kitchens and works well in a galley kitchen. The carrying surface should measure about 16 by 16 inches (40 by 40 cm). You can find a good wooden peel for around $15.

The peel can also serve as a proofing surface during the final rise. Before using, dust the peel with flour or cornmeal to allow the loaf to easily slide onto and off the stone.

A **food thermometer** is good for testing the temperature of the dough or even the doneness of a loaf. To determine whether your bread is done, insert a food thermometer into the center of the loaf; if it registers over 212°F (100°C), your bread is finished baking. You can find food thermometers in the gadget section of most grocery stores.

A **bread lame or razor blade** is useful for scoring the tops of formed loaves. Scores are cuts in the loaf made just prior to baking to allow for a more controlled expansion of the loaf and to release the moisture in the dough. The scores or slashes also give the bread a distinctive appearance.

A **cooling rack** is helpful. This doesn't have to be fancy. A raised wire rack on the counter will serve the purpose.

A good **serrated knife** can be used to cut dough as well as baked bread.

Both a metal and a plastic **dough scraper** are helpful for mixing, dividing, scraping, and cleanup.

THE HEARTH OVEN

There's no way around it. A hearth oven really makes the difference when it comes to good artisan bread. Sadly, not everyone has the money or space for such an item. If you are inclined to build a hearth oven, check out the book *The Bread Builders: Hearth Loaves and Masonry Ovens* by Daniel Wing and Alan Scott, which provides clear instructions on how to build a hearth oven in your own backyard.

CONVERTING YOUR OVEN TO A HEARTH OVEN FOR REBAR STEAM BAKING

The good news is that you can also turn your kitchen oven into a hearth oven. To convert your oven into a hearth oven, purchase a half-size hotel stainless-steel pan measuring 10 ⅜ by 12 ¾ inches (26 by 32 cm) with a depth of at least 2 inches (5 cm), or simply use a broiling pan. Please note, it *cannot* be glass, or it could shatter.

Next, purchase 10 rebar—steel reinforcing bars used to reinforce concrete—that are 12 inches long and ¾ inch in diameter (30 by 2 cm) to fit your pan. You can find rebar this size at a hardware or big-box store like Home Depot, Lowe's, or Menards. Put the tray with the rebar on the rack closest to the bottom of the oven and below the rack that has your baking stone. The purpose of the rebar is to have something to retain heat to create steam. Steam prevents the loaf from forming a crust too early in the baking process.

When the loaf is ready to go into the oven, use your oven peel to put the proofed loaf onto the baking stone and then add about ½ cup (120 ml) of water to the pan with the rebar. Quickly close the oven door to prevent the steam from escaping the oven. The steam created by the wet rebar will allow the loaf to expand and will contribute to the quick expansion of bread when placed in a hot, moist oven, known as the oven jump or oven spring.

Be sure to wear oven gloves and a long-sleeved shirt to avoid steam burns.

HOMEMADE PROOF BOX

One common issue with artisan baking is temperature. It is critical that your starter is kept between 72 and 78°F (22 and 25.5°C). Any warm place in your house should work well, but for especially drafty houses, this might be an issue. Another way to maintain this is to use a simple, homemade proofing box. You will need a 50-quart (47.3 liter) cooler, a 180-watt light bulb and light base, and a programmable outlet thermostat. Connect the light to the programmable outlet thermostat, place in the cooler, and plug into an outlet. Program your thermostat to the range of 72 to 78°F (22 to 25.5°C). The thermostat will turn the light on when it drops below 72°F (22°C). If you are having trouble getting proper fermentation in your starters, this cheap and simple homemade proof box will create more control in your baking.

These are the tools that you will most likely use in your baking adventures. As you go along, you will find a tool or two that will be most helpful to your own unique way of making bread.

ARTISAN INGREDIENTS

The ingredients for artisan bread are simple—flour, water, and salt—and, of course, your starter made from flour and water. These ingredients are widely available, but there are many different varieties.

To create a good-quality bread, you must start with a good-quality **flour**. Try to make sure that the flour is unbleached and has no additives. The vitamin enrichment requirements in white flour vary from state to state, and this is OK if there are no other additives or bleaching. You want this bread to be as natural and chemical-free as possible.

The protein content or gluten in wheat provides the structure in bread. We prefer to use flour milled from hard red winter wheat with a protein content around 12 percent. Brands that meet this standard include: Central Milling's Organic Artisan Bakers Craft, King Arthur Unbleached All-Purpose, Heartland Mill's Strong Bread Flour, General Mills's Harvest King European Artisan Bread Flour, Enriched and Unbleached. Going forward, we will refer to these flours as **bread flour**.

Water is everywhere, and most tap water is fine to use in bread. Some areas of the country have tap water that is heavily chlorinated, which will kill the good bacteria and yeast in the starters. If that's your situation, use bottled water instead.

Salt helps the flavor in bread. It is also helps to control fermentation. I recommend fine kosher or sea salt, but any salt will work.

Beyond the basic ingredients for creating the loaf, there are flavor additions. Typically, you'll want to stay away from fresh produce in exchange for cooked or dried vegetables. For example, you'll want sun-dried rather than fresh tomatoes, onions sautéed until golden rather than raw, and roasted garlic instead of fresh. However, when using herbs, you will want fresh, pungent herbs like rosemary and thyme. Other strong flavors, like aged cheeses, nuts, and seeds, will work great with these breads.

Now that you understand the tools and ingredients needed to make the bread, let's get acquainted with the natural yeasts in the air to make the starters.

CHAPTER TWO

NATURAL STARTERS
AND BREAD BAKING

A NATURAL STARTER IS the method of natural leavening that has been around since the beginning of civilization. Early peoples discovered that when a mixture of flour and water was left to set for some time, the mixture would magically change. The mix would bubble and rise, becoming lighter, more flavorful, and easier to digest. What was happening was that bacteria and yeast from the atmosphere were joining the mix, causing the process known today as fermentation.

It was not until the mid-1800s that Louis Pasteur discovered that microorganisms were creating the alchemy that made starters. These starters are products of two types of microorganisms: wild yeast and bacteria. The yeast and bacteria are drawn from the air and from the flour itself. If the starter is fed and watered, it can survive for years, adding flavor and raising your dough time after time.

Like beer, wine, and cheese, bread is a product of fermentation. In his book *The Art of Fermentation*, Sandor Ellix Katz describes fermentation as "the flavorful space between fresh and rotten." The starter is a microecosystem of flour and water inhabited by yeast and bacteria. Three important things happen simultaneously in the starter fermentation: The dough expands, the starter becomes more acidic, and microbes reproduce.

The yeast feeds on the carbohydrates from the flour and turns them into carbon dioxide (CO_2) and alcohol, which causes the dough to expand. Although most of the alcohol bakes out of the bread in the oven, the alcohol produces unique flavors that remain and help enhance the final flavor of the bread.

The bacteria also feed on the carbohydrates but produce acids that flavor the bread and lower its pH. The pH indicates the amount of acidity present in a substance. The acidity is what gives the bread its sour and tangy flavor.

Next, the microbes reproduce, allowing the starter to ripen. When the starter has fully ripened, it yields both the new starter for continued feeding and the starter that will be used and baked into bread. A fully fermented or ripe starter has a yeast and bacteria count of approximately 18 million CFU (Colony Forming Units) per gram. A piece of starter inoculates the next-generation starter with yeast and bacteria by mixing 3 parts ripe starter, 10 parts flour, and 5 parts water; this is also known as feeding the starter. In this feeding, the yeast and bacteria cell count are diluted. After 6 to 10 hours at room temperature, the yeast and bacteria reproduce, replenishing the population back to the original count. During this process, the starter will more than double in size.

When you first create your starter, it may seem like nothing is happening,

Day 1   Day 2   Day 3

Day 4   Day 5

but trust me, things are. During the first couple of days, many unseen things occur. The yeast and bacteria from the flour and air are beginning their feast. Around the second or third day, you might see some movement or expansion of the starter. By the fifth day, the starter should have doubled in size, filling the liter container. During the five days, the yeast and bacteria count goes from 5 hundred CFU to 18 million CFU. Many factors affect fermentation, so there are no absolute times and patience is important. It helps to remember that even if you think nothing is happening, something is. However, if by Day 3 you have not seen any growth on your starter, you should be concerned. One common issue is temperature. It is critical that your starter is kept between 72 and 78°F (22 and 25.5°C). Any warm place in your house works great. For especially drafty houses, this might be an issue. Another way to maintain this temperature is to use a simple, homemade proofing box (see page 20 for instructions).

Beyond the wonder of fermentation, there are other benefits to using a starter in the process of bread baking. Some research has shown positive physiological responses to sourdough made with a natural starter. Those involved in the study showed lower blood glucose levels after eating sourdough bread; that positive response lasted through the next meal and several hours later. In other words, sourdough bread made from starter has a lower glycemic index than bread made with commercial yeast. The glycemic index measures how high and how quickly blood sugar spikes after eating a food. People with diabetes or who are at risk of diabetes will be happy with this choice.

Further, starters also enhance our absorption of certain minerals in the flour by helping break down the acid that inhibits mineral absorption. In addition, the bacteria and wild yeast in the culture work to predigest the starches, making the bread more easily digestible.

Both the acetic acid and the lactic acid that are produced in the starter help preserve the bread by inhibiting the growth of mold. Good artisan bread can keep anywhere from a few days to over a week depending on how the bread is stored. If the loaf is going to be eaten within three days, it is best kept on your countertop, unwrapped. The natural protection of a crusty exterior will preserve the soft interior crumb. For longer storage, wrap the loaf and store in the freezer. When ready to enjoy, thaw at room temperature and reheat in a 400°F (205°C) oven for 3 to 5 minutes.

Now that you have a better understanding of starters, you are ready to make your own. This book addresses three different kinds of starters and a packaged yeast ferment known as biga, all four of which are known as pre-ferments. We will be looking at a stiff San Francisco sourdough starter; a softer pre-ferment known as levain; and a rye starter, used for baking rye flour-based breads. Biga, although not technically a natural starter, is dry and thick, with a slightly nutty taste, and is made fresh every day, using a small amount of instant yeast (we like SAF brand) in a thick dough, which is then allowed to ferment for 12 to 16 hours to develop flavor.

These starters are not difficult to make and share many similar steps. However, some, like the Levain (page 31), require more attention to keep growing.

CREATING YOUR SAN FRANCISCO
SOURDOUGH STARTER

Find a 1-liter container with an easily removable lid for your starter. A lid that slides or pops off will be best, as it will allow for the surprise expansion of the starter, which may occur at any time. This container will be used for both creating and storing the starter.

DAY	TIME	INGREDIENTS	AMOUNT		NOTES
Day 1	8:00 a.m.	Bread flour	1 cup 1 tablespoon 2 teaspoons	150 g	On **Day 1**, mix the flour and water together on low speed for 4 minutes, until you have a smooth liquid mass like pancake batter. Place in the 1-liter container. Leave, covered with cloth or plastic, at room temperature to ferment for 24 hours.
		Water 78–82°F (26–28°C)	½ cup 2 tablespoons	150 ml	
Day 2	8:00 a.m.	Starter	¾ cup 1 tablespoon	150 g	• On the **morning of Day 2,** the starter is your previous day's dough. Measure out ¾ cup and 1 tablespoon (150 g) Day 1 starter and discard any remaining starter. Mix the starter with the flour and water on low speed for 4 minutes, until you have a smooth liquid mass. Return the mixture to the 1-liter container. Leave, covered with cloth or plastic, at room temperature to ferment for 12 hours.
		Bread flour	1 cup 1 tablespoon 2 teaspoons	150 g	
		Water 78–82°F (26–28°C)	½ cup 2 tablespoons	150 ml	
	8:00 p.m.	Starter	¾ cup 1 tablespoon	150 g	• On the **evening of Day 2,** repeat the mixing process using ¾ cup and 1 tablespoon (150 g) of the starter from the morning of Day 2 with the flour and water, and discard any remaining starter. Repeat the mixing and storing following the morning instructions.
		Bread flour	1 cup 1 tablespoon 2 teaspoons	150 g	
		Water 78–82°F (26–28°C)	½ cup 2 tablespoons	150 ml	

DAY	TIME	INGREDIENTS	AMOUNT		NOTES
Day 3	8:00 a.m.	Starter	¾ cup 1 tablespoon	150 g	• On the **morning of Day 3,** the starter is your previous day's evening dough. Measure out ¾ cup and 1 tablespoon (150 g) Day 2 starter and discard any remaining starter. Mix the starter with the flour and water on low speed for 4 minutes, until you have a smooth liquid mass. Return the mixture to the 1-liter container. Leave, covered with cloth or plastic, at room temperature to ferment for 12 hours.
		Bread flour	1 cup 1 tablespoon 2 teaspoons	150 g	
		Water 78–82°F (26–28°C)	½ cup 2 tablespoons	150 ml	
	8:00 p.m.	Starter	¾ cup 1 tablespoon	150 g	• On the **evening of Day 3,** repeat the mixing process using ¾ cup and 1 tablespoon (150 g) of the starter from the morning of Day 3 with the flour and water, and discard any remaining starter. Repeat the mixing and storing following the morning instructions.
		Bread flour	1 cup 1 tablespoon 2 teaspoons	150 g	
		Water 78–82°F (26–28°C)	½ cup 2 tablespoons	150 ml	

On Day 4 in creating San Francisco Sourdough, the starter transitions to a stiff starter. The first three days have more water to enhance the success of creating the starter. On Day 4, the starter transitions to a lower water level and is more stiff than the previous days. Note the change in water and flour amounts. Measure the ingredients carefully.

DAY	TIME	INGREDIENTS	AMOUNT		NOTES
Day 4	8:00 a.m.	Starter	1 cup 1 teaspoon	187 g	• On the **morning of Day 4,** the starter is your previous day's evening dough. Measure out 1 cup and 1 teaspoon (187 g) Day 3 starter and discard any remaining starter. Mix the starter with the flour and water on low speed for 4 minutes, until you have a smooth liquid mass. Return the mixture to the 1-liter container. Leave, covered with cloth or plastic, at room temperature to ferment for 12 hours.
		Bread flour	1 ⅓ cups 2 teaspoons	187 g	
		Water 78–82°F (26–28°C)	⅓ cup 1 teaspoon	86 ml	
	8:00 p.m.	Starter	¾ cup 1 tablespoon	150 g	• On the **evening of Day 4,** repeat the mixing process using ¾ cup and 1 tablespoon (150 g) of the starter from the morning of Day 4 with the flour and water, and discard any remaining starter. Repeat the mixing and storing following the morning instructions.
		Bread flour	1 ½ cups 2 tablespoons	200 g	
		Water 78–82°F (26–28°C)	⅓ cup 1 tablespoon 1 teaspoon	100 ml	

DAY	TIME	INGREDIENTS	AMOUNT		NOTES
		Starter	⅓ cup 1 tablespoon	75 g	On the **morning of Day 5,** the starter is your previous day's evening dough. Measure out ⅓ cup and 1 tablespoon (75 g) Day 4 starter and discard any remaining starter. Mix the starter with the flour and water and mix on low speed for 4 minutes, until you have a smooth, stiffer mass, like bread dough. Return the mixture to the 1-liter container. Leave, covered with cloth or plastic, at room temperature to ferment for 12 hours. Then place in the refrigerator until ready to bake.
Day 5	8:00 a.m.	Bread flour	1 ¾ cups	240 g	
		Water 78–82°F (26–28°C)	½ cup 1 tablespoon	135 ml	

MAINTAINING THE STARTER

An important thing to remember is that this starter is a living organism and therefore needs to be fed. Without regular feeding, the starter—like any living thing—will die. The feeding doesn't need to be hard and fast, but it does need to be done on a regular basis.

Starter	⅓ cup 2 teaspoons	70 g
Bread flour	1 ¾ cups	240 g
Water 78–82°F (26–28°C)	½ cup 1 tablespoon 1 teaspoon	140 ml

Measure out ⅓ cup and 2 teaspoons (70 grams) of the starter and mix with 1 ¾ cups (240 g) flour and ½ cup, 1 tablespoon, and 1 teaspoon (140 ml) water. Discard any remaining starter. Allow the mixture to ferment at room temperature for 8 to 10 hours, then refrigerate. Feeding couldn't be simpler.

Your starter needs to be regularly fed, at least every 4 days, but preferably more often and daily, if possible. If you will be gone for a time, the starter can be frozen by placing it in a sealed container in your freezer. At the time you wish to use it again, simply thaw until it can be mixed and follow the procedure for feeding. If the starter seems lackadaisical, repeat the feeding process (maintaining the starter) until it has become healthy and rises to the top of the liter container within 10 hours. After a long stint out, in the refrigerator or freezing, the starter may not respond to resuscitation. If this happens, discard the

starter and start over from scratch. There's plenty of bacteria in the air and the flour, so new starters are just waiting to be created.

Pain au levain naturel. It is often simply referred to as levain. *Levain* is the French term for a mixture of flour and water that has been colonized by yeasts and bacteria. As with the San Francisco sourdough starter, the bacteria and yeast consume the carbohydrates and consequently need to be fed continuously so they will always have a source of energy. With regular feedings, the levain ecosystem becomes more stable and stronger.

As bakers experimented over millennia, it became evident that different proportions of water, flour, and previous starter yielded different starters. Adding more flour and less water produced the stiff San Francisco sourdough starter. Adding more water and less flour produced a more fluid style of starter often referred to as poolish. Traditional levain was somewhere between the two extremes. Today, artisan bakers tend to favor a more liquid levain, and that's the style you will be working with.

Breads made with starters may date back to 3000 BC. The tradition of the current *pain au levain naturel* of Poilâne bakery in Paris dates to AD 1600. In fact, it predates baguettes, which started about 1920. Although it is the name of the leavening method, people frequently will also use the word *levain* to refer to a rustic French bread made with this starter.

WHAT'S INVOLVED IN A LEVAIN STARTER?

The same process used for the sourdough starter is repeated with the levain, except for using different ratios of flour to water, and adding whole wheat and rye flour. The levain will begin moving slowly, but be patient and confident that the process has begun. Beginning on Day 2, you'll feed the levain twice a day. Feeding the levain allows the microbe ecosystem to grow. A good, mature levain should be elastic and start to double in size after 12 hours of fermentation.

As a baker, you can tell how the starter is doing just by looking. For the levain, you'll need a 1-liter container, just like you used for the San Francisco sourdough starter, as it will allow for growth even when refrigerated. When you first mix the flour and water for the levain, you will see that only a small portion of the container is filled. As you approach the end of the fermentation period, the mixture will rise to near the top of the container.

Continue to feed the levain water and flour, mix the ingredients, and allow to ferment for 12 hours. This process is repeated for 5 days until the levain is mature; it will look active and have a tangy aroma. Once the levain has matured, feed the levain daily to ensure its health and fermentation. The daily feeding of the starter allows for it to be used directly in the bread without additional steps.

Remember that the factors of the kind of flour, time and temperature of the fermentation, and water level in the dough will affect the levain and final loaf. This French traditional method of bread making is meant to yield a flavorful but less sour loaf of bread. Farm to Market's *pain au levain naturel* is our French Farm Loaf (page 80).

MAKING YOUR LEVAIN

Making levain is a commitment because this starter is best fed every day. Although it doesn't take much time to do, the fact that you must do it each day can be intimidating. Fit it into your schedule according to what works best for you.

The rye and wheat flours added in the first four days help create the rustic flavor and provide enzymes and bacteria to the levain.

DAY	TIME	INGREDIENTS	AMOUNT		NOTES
Day 1	8:00 a.m.	Rye flour	1 tablespoon 2 teaspoons	10 g	On **Day 1,** mix the flours and water together on low for 4 minutes, until you have a smooth mass resembling pancake batter. Place in the 1-liter container. Leave, covered with cloth or plastic, at room temperature to ferment for 24 hours.
		Whole wheat flour	2 tablespoons 2 teaspoons	20 g	
		Bread flour	¾ cup 2 tablespoons	120 g	
		Water 78–82°F (26–28°C)	½ cup 2 tablespoons	150 ml	

DAY	TIME	INGREDIENTS	AMOUNT		NOTES
Day 2	8:00 a.m.	Starter	¾ cup 1 tablespoon	150 g	• On the **morning of Day 2,** the starter is your previous day's dough. Measure out ¾ cup and 1 tablespoon (150 g) of Day 1 starter and discard any remaining starter. Mix the starter together with the flours and water on low for 4 minutes, until you have a smooth mass resembling pancake batter. Return the mixture to the 1-liter container. Leave, covered with cloth or plastic, at room temperature to ferment for 12 hours.
		Rye flour	1 tablespoon 2 teaspoons	10 g	
		Whole wheat flour	2 tablespoons 2 teaspoons	20 g	
		Bread flour	¾ cup 2 tablespoons	120 g	
		Water 78–82°F (26–28°C)	½ cup 2 tablespoons	150 ml	
	8:00 p.m.	Starter	¾ cup 1 tablespoon	150 g	• On the **evening of Day 2,** repeat the mixing process using ¾ cup and 1 tablespoon (150 g) of the starter from the morning of Day 2 with the flours and water, and discard any remaining starter. Repeat the mixing and storing following the morning instructions.
		Rye flour	1 tablespoon 2 teaspoons	10 g	
		Whole wheat flour	2 tablespoons 2 teaspoons	20 g	
		Bread flour	¾ cup 2 tablespoons	120 g	
		Water 78–82°F (26–28°C)	½ cup 2 tablespoons	150 ml	

DAY	TIME	INGREDIENTS	AMOUNT		NOTES
Day 3	8:00 a.m.	Starter	¾ cup 1 tablespoon	150 g	• On the **morning of Day 3,** the starter is your previous day's evening dough. Measure out ¾ cup and 1 tablespoon (150 g) of Day 2 starter and discard any remaining starter. Mix the starter together with the flours and water on low for 4 minutes, until you have a smooth mass resembling pancake batter. Return the mixture to the 1-liter container. Leave, covered with cloth or plastic, at room temperature to ferment for 12 hours.
		Rye flour	1 tablespoon 2 teaspoons	10 g	
		Whole wheat flour	2 tablespoons 2 teaspoons	20 g	
		Bread flour	¾ cup 2 tablespoons	120 g	
		Water 78–82°F (26–28°C)	½ cup 2 tablespoons	150 ml	
	8:00 p.m.	Starter	¾ cup 1 tablespoon	150 g	• On the **evening of Day 3,** repeat the mixing process using ¾ cup and 1 tablespoon (150 g) of the starter from the morning of Day 3 with the flours and water, and discard any remaining starter. Repeat the mixing and storing following the morning instructions.
		Rye flour	1 tablespoon 2 teaspoons	10 g	
		Whole wheat flour	2 tablespoons 2 teaspoons	20 g	
		Bread flour	¾ cup 2 tablespoons	120 g	
		Water 78–82°F (26–28°C)	½ cup 2 tablespoons	150 ml	

DAY	TIME	INGREDIENTS	AMOUNT		NOTES
Day 4	8:00 a.m.	Starter	¾ cup 1 tablespoon	150 g	• On the **morning of Day 4,** the starter is your previous day's evening dough. Measure out ¾ cup and 1 tablespoon (150 g) of Day 3 starter and discard any remaining starter. Mix the starter together with the flours and water on low for 4 minutes, until you have a smooth mass resembling pancake batter. Return the mixture to the 1-liter container. Leave, covered with cloth or plastic, at room temperature to ferment for 12 hours.
		Rye flour	1 tablespoon 2 teaspoons	10 g	
		Whole wheat flour	2 tablespoons 2 teaspoons	20 g	
		Bread flour	¾ cup 2 tablespoons	120 g	
		Water 78–82°F (26–28°C)	½ cup 2 tablespoons	150 ml	
	8:00 p.m.	Starter	¾ cup 1 tablespoon	150 g	• On the **evening of Day 4,** repeat the mixing process using ¾ cup and 1 tablespoon (150 g) of the starter from the morning of Day 4 with the flours and water, and discard any remaining starter. Repeat the mixing and storing following the morning instructions.
		Rye flour	1 tablespoon 2 teaspoons	10 g	
		Whole wheat flour	2 tablespoons 2 teaspoons	20 g	
		Bread flour	¾ cup 2 tablespoons	120 g	
		Water 78–82°F (26–28°C)	½ cup 2 tablespoons	150 ml	

DAY	TIME	INGREDIENTS	AMOUNT		NOTES
Day 5	8:00 a.m.	Starter	¾ cup 1 tablespoon	150 g	• On the **morning of Day 5,** the starter is your previous day's evening dough. Measure out ¾ cup and 1 tablespoon (150 g) of Day 4 starter and discard any remaining starter. Mix the starter together with the flours and water on low for 4 minutes, until you have a smooth mass resembling pancake batter. Return the mixture to the 1-liter container. Leave, covered with cloth or plastic, at room temperature to ferment for 12 hours.
		Rye flour	1 tablespoon 2 teaspoons	10 g	
		Whole wheat flour	2 tablespoons 2 teaspoons	20 g	
		Bread flour	¾ cup 2 tablespoons	120 g	
		Water 78–82°F (26–28°C)	½ cup 2 tablespoons	150 ml	
	8:00 p.m.	Starter	¾ cup 1 tablespoon	150 g	• On the **evening of Day 5,** repeat the mixing process using ¾ cup and 1 tablespoon (150 g) of the starter from the morning of Day 5 with the flours and water, and discard any remaining starter. Repeat the mixing and storing following the morning instructions.
		Rye flour	1 tablespoon 2 teaspoons	10 g	
		Whole wheat flour	2 tablespoons 2 teaspoons	20 g	
		Bread flour	¾ cup 2 tablespoons	120 g	
		Water 78–82°F (26–28°C)	½ cup 2 tablespoons	150 ml	

On the **morning of Day 6**, your starter is complete and ready to begin helping you make loaves of levain. If you will be gone for a time, the starter can be frozen by placing it in a sealed container in your freezer. At the time you wish to use it again, simply thaw until it can be worked and follow the procedure for the feeding. If the starter seems lackadaisical, repeat the feeding process until it has reawakened completely. After a long stint of disuse or after freezing, the starter may not respond to resuscitation. If this happens, discard the starter and start from scratch.

MAINTAINING THE LEVAIN

Measure out ¾ cup and 1 tablespoon (150 g) of the levain and mix with 1 tablespoon and 2 teaspoons (10 g) rye flour, 2 tablespoons and 2 teaspoons (20 g) whole wheat flour, ¾ cup and 2 tablespoons (120 g) bread flour, and ½ cup and 2 tablespoons (150 ml) water. Discard any remaining starter. Allow the mixture to ferment at room temperature for 8 to 10 hours, then refrigerate. Your levain should be fed more frequently than the sourdough starter, about every other day, to be at its best. If you intend to bake a bread with levain, it would be good to cycle through two feedings before making the dough to have it at optimum activity.

Starter	¾ cup 1 tablespoon	150 g
Rye flour	1 tablespoon 2 teaspoons	10 g
Whole wheat flour	2 tablespoons 2 teaspoons	20 g
Bread flour	¾ cup 2 tablespoons	120 g
Water 78–82°F (26–28°C)	½ cup 2 tablespoons	150 ml

RYE STARTER

For this starter, as with the other starters, water and rye and wheat flours are allowed to ferment and grow for a specified period of time and then used to leaven each loaf of bread.

Rye is a grain that is often overlooked, but it fed people as far back as 13,000 years ago, in early settlements in Northern Europe (Russia, Germany, Poland, and Scandinavia). When other grains failed to grow because of drought or freezing weather, rye flourished. It was particularly plentiful in the cool, wet Northern European plains, often popping up in fields unannounced.

In the Middle Ages, white bread was the preferred bread for the elite and, as a result, rye bread became known as the bread of peasants. One contributing factor was that rye flour was not easy to work with. Rye bread required more time for rising and baking.

Rye breads are relatively unpopular in the United States, although they celebrated a slight resurgence in the 1990s. One of the reasons for rye's lack of popularity may be that when immigrants arrived from Europe, they gradually began to do away with the old ways that included the baking of rye bread. Another contributor was the fact that bakers switched to yeast instead of starter and began to incorporate a larger percentage of unbleached bread flour into the mix. This different baking approach significantly changed the baking of rye breads. Recipes no longer required slow baking with sour starter as the leavening method. Commercial yeast was added to a combination of rye and white flours, which resulted in a lighter, more palatable loaf for people not accustomed to the flavor of heavy rye bread.

Pumpernickel bread is a dark rye bread normally made with coarse rye flour. The dark color was due to longer baking times (16 hours) in steam chambers at lower temperatures (220 to 270°F, or 104 to 132°C). Most American pumpernickel bread has added coloring to achieve the dark brown shade. German rules require true rye bread to contain at least 90 percent rye flour. Farm to Market Bread Company bakes beautiful and tasty rye bread, using 70 percent wheat and 30 percent rye flour and a rye starter that both leavens and flavors. Let's learn how that starter can be made at home and used to make some truly beautiful and varied loaves of rye bread.

There's a saying in Germany that people don't care which side their bread is buttered on, or whether it is buttered at all, as long as it is made from rye. Rye got its start as an invasive weed that contaminated other fields, but over the years it has proven itself to be useful. It can grow in very poor soils and tolerate less-than-ideal conditions, such as less sun, more rain, and even drought. Bread made from rye keeps longer, and to some, it tastes head and shoulders better than white bread. The loaves are moist and when you bite into them you feel as if you are eating something full of history. It all begins with rye starter, referred to as rye sour. Rye sour, as the name implies, will be sour in smell and tangy in taste when fully developed.

Before you begin to make your starter, you will need a 1-liter container that will serve as the starter's home. This is where you will store the starter between uses and where it will return when it has been fed. Make sure the lid can easily be removed so that it can accommodate any expansion the starter may experience.

CREATING YOUR RYE STARTER

DAY	TIME	INGREDIENTS	AMOUNT		NOTES
Day 1	8:00 a.m.	Rye flour	⅓ cup 2 tablespoons 1 teaspoon	50 g	On **Day 1,** mix the flours and water together on low for 4 minutes, until you have a smooth mass resembling pancake batter. Place in the 1-liter container. Leave, covered with cloth or plastic, at room temperature to ferment for 24 hours.
		Bread flour	¾ cup	100 g	
		Water 78–82°F (26–28°C)	½ cup 2 tablespoons	150 ml	

DAY	TIME	INGREDIENTS	AMOUNT		NOTES
Day 2	8:00 a.m.	Starter	¾ cup 1 tablespoon	150 g	• On the **morning of Day 2,** the starter is your previous day's dough. Measure out ¾ cup and 1 tablespoon (150 g) of Day 1 starter and discard any remaining starter. Mix the starter together with the flours and water on low for 4 minutes, until you have a smooth mass resembling pancake batter. Return the mixture to the 1-liter container. Leave, covered with cloth or plastic, at room temperature to ferment for 12 hours.
		Rye flour	⅓ cup 2 tablespoons 1 teaspoon	50 g	
		Bread flour	¾ cup	100 g	
		Water 78–82°F (26–28°C)	½ cup 2 tablespoons	150 ml	
	8:00 p.m.	Starter	¾ cup 1 tablespoon	150 g	• On the **evening of Day 2,** repeat the mixing process using ¾ cup and 1 tablespoon (150 g) of the starter from the morning of Day 2 with the flours and water, and discard any remaining starter. Repeat the mixing and storing following the morning instructions.
		Rye flour	⅓ cup 2 tablespoons 1 teaspoon	50 g	
		Bread flour	¾ cup	100 g	
		Water 78–82°F (26–28°C)	½ cup 2 tablespoons	150 ml	

DAY	TIME	INGREDIENTS	AMOUNT		NOTES
Day 3	8:00 a.m.	Starter	¾ cup 1 tablespoon	150 g	• On the **morning of Day 3,** the starter is your previous day's evening dough. Measure out ¾ cup and 1 tablespoon (150 g) of Day 2 starter and discard any remaining starter. Mix the starter together with the flours and water on low for 4 minutes, until you have a smooth mass resembling pancake batter. Return the mixture to the 1-liter container. Leave, covered with cloth or plastic, at room temperature to ferment for 12 hours.
		Rye flour	⅓ cup 2 tablespoons 1 teaspoon	50 g	
		Bread flour	¾ cup	100 g	
		Water 78–82°F (26–28°C)	½ cup 2 tablespoons	150 ml	
	8:00 p.m.	Starter	¾ cup 1 tablespoon	150 g	• On the **evening of Day 3,** repeat the mixing process using ¾ cup and 1 tablespoon (150 g) of the starter from the morning of Day 3 with the flours and water, and discard any remaining starter. Repeat the mixing and storing following the morning instructions.
		Rye flour	⅓ cup 2 tablespoons 1 teaspoon	50 g	
		Bread flour	¾ cup	100 g	
		Water 78–82°F (26–28°C)	½ cup 2 tablespoons	150 ml	

DAY	TIME	INGREDIENTS	AMOUNT		NOTES
Day 4	8:00 a.m.	Starter	¾ cup 1 tablespoon	150 g	• On the **morning of Day 4,** the starter is your previous day's evening dough. Measure out ¾ cup and 1 tablespoon (150 g) of Day 3 starter and discard any remaining starter. Mix the starter together with the flours and water on low for 4 minutes, until you have a smooth mass resembling pancake batter. Return the mixture to the 1-liter container. Leave, covered with cloth or plastic, at room temperature to ferment for 12 hours.
		Rye flour	⅓ cup 2 tablespoons 1 teaspoon	50 g	
		Bread flour	¾ cup	100 g	
		Water 78–82°F (26–28°C)	½ cup 2 tablespoons	150 ml	
	8:00 p.m.	Starter	¾ cup 1 tablespoon	150 g	• On the **evening of Day 4**, repeat the mixing process using ¾ cup and 1 tablespoon (150 g) of the starter from the morning of Day 4 with the flours and water, and discard any remaining starter. Repeat the mixing and storing following the morning instructions.
		Rye flour	⅓ cup 2 tablespoons 1 teaspoon	50 g	
		Bread flour	¾ cup	100 g	
		Water 78–82°F (26–28°C)	½ cup 2 tablespoons	150 ml	
Day 5	8:00 a.m.	Starter	¾ cup 1 tablespoon	150 g	• On the **morning of Day 5,** the starter is your previous day's evening dough. Measure out ¾ cup and 1 tablespoon (150 g) of Day 4 starter and discard any remaining starter. Mix the starter together with the flours and water on low for 4 minutes, until you have a smooth mass resembling pancake batter. Return the mixture to the 1-liter container. Leave, covered with cloth or plastic, at room temperature to ferment for 12 hours.
		Rye flour	⅓ cup 2 tablespoons 1 teaspoon	50 g	
		Bread flour	¾ cup	100 g	
		Water 78–82°F (26–28°C)	½ cup 2 tablespoons	150 ml	
	8:00 p.m.	Starter	¾ cup 1 tablespoon	150 g	• On the **evening of Day 5**, repeat the mixing process using ¾ cup and 1 tablespoon (150 g) of the starter from the morning of Day 5 with the flours and water, and discard any remaining starter. Repeat the mixing and storing following the morning instructions.
		Rye flour	⅓ cup 2 tablespoons 1 teaspoon	50 g	
		Bread flour	¾ cup	100 g	
		Water 78–82°F (26–28°C)	½ cup 2 tablespoons	150 ml	

DAY	TIME	INGREDIENTS	AMOUNT	NOTES

On the **morning of Day 6,** your starter is complete and ready to begin helping you make loaves of rye bread. If you will be gone for a time, the starter can be frozen by placing it in a sealed container in your freezer. At the time you wish to use it again, simply thaw until it can be worked and follow the procedure for the feeding. If the starter seems lackadaisical, repeat the feeding process until it has reawakened completely. After a long stint of disuse or after freezing, the starter may not respond to resuscitation. If this happens, discard the starter and start from scratch.

MAINTAINING THE RYE STARTER

Your rye starter, like the other starters, needs to be fed regularly. To feed and refresh, measure ¾ cup and 1 tablespoon (150 g) starter, ⅓ cup plus 2 tablespoons and 1 teaspoon (50 g) rye flour, ¾ cup (100 g) bread flour, and ½ cup and 2 tablespoons (150 g) water. Discard the rest of the remaining starter. Mix and allow to ferment in a 1-liter container for the day, basically 8 to 12 hours, in your kitchen, then refrigerate. Your rye starter should be fed every 4 days to keep it at its best.

Starter	¾ cup 1 tablespoon	150 g
Rye flour	⅓ cup 2 tablespoons 1 teaspoon	50 g
Bread flour	¾ cup	100 g
Water 78–82°F (26–28°C)	½ cup 2 tablespoons	150 ml

CHAPTER THREE

EIGHT STEPS TO BAKING
ARTISAN BREAD THE FARM TO MARKET WAY

THIS CHAPTER OUTLINES ALL THE STEPS REQUIRED to make any loaf of bread leavened with a natural starter. Each step is very important and should be followed with care. You will notice that there are comments in some sections that refer to a starter. This is done so you will see how little the basic recipe changes from starter to starter. The most important difference to note is the proofing times.

STEP 1: MEASURING

Read through the entire recipe. It contains simple ingredients: the starter, the flour, the water, and the salt. For the bread to have a good start, it is important that all the ingredients are properly weighed and prepared. We give you the weights in each recipe, but you do the weighing using a small digital kitchen scale. Take out your scale and weigh the ingredients.

First, measure out the amount of fresh starter you need. Fresh starter has been fed and fermented for 8 hours. Weigh the starter carefully and then set aside.

Next, weigh the flour. Put the mixing bowl on the scale and select the tare or zero function. The tare or zero function is used to subtract the weight of the empty container, so the scale will show zero, allowing you to measure only the weight of the ingredient. Add flour until the scale indicates that you have the correct weight of flour for the recipe.

Measure the salt. After placing a small container on the scale, select tare or zero. Once at zero, add salt to the container until you reach the proper measured amount indicated by the recipe.

Next, measure the water. You'll need a large container for the water. Once again, place the container on the scale and select the tare or zero function. Then add water to the container. The temperature of the water should be room temperature, between 78 and 82°F (26 and 28°C). If you don't have a food thermometer, a good indicator of the correct temperature is that the water is warm to the touch.

In addition to measuring out the basic ingredients, you will also measure the ingredients for the sponge (for sourdough) and the other ingredients for the dough to follow, which vary by recipe.

Step 1A: Preparing the Sponge (for Sourdough Breads and Black Russian Rye Only)

Preparing the sponge is a straightforward process: You simply mix the sponge ingredients together into a cohesive mass. If using a stand mixer, mix for 3 to 5 minutes on low speed. If mixing by hand, mix until the ingredients come together in one mass. Mix just until the ingredients are brought together into a smooth mass, much as if you were preparing a pancake batter. Note: It is important not to overmix the sponge. Leave in the bowl, cover, and allow to rise for between 3 to 5 hours at room temperature.

STEP 2: MIXING THE DOUGH

One benefit of using our hands is to become familiar with the changes to the dough to achieve the desired consistency. You need to train your hands to recognize when the dough is fully mixed and when the gluten has reached its best potential. Your hands will also tell you if the dough is too moist or dry, springy, or dull. In *A Passion for Bread*, Lionel Vatinet writes, "Your fingers are your memory." During the time of baking apprenticeships, French apprentices had to learn first by hand before they could go to the mixers. This was done so that they would become more familiar with the dough and hence were better able to understand it, making for better bread in the end. Whether you choose to mix by hand or use an electric mixer, do what is comfortable for you. I find mixing by hand to be more satisfying because I can feel the dough and feel how it changes. Regardless of whether you mix by hand or with a mixer, it is important that you take time to feel the dough and learn to read it well.

Mixing by Hand

Use your hands to incorporate all of the ingredients by mixing with your hands or dough scraper until you have a smooth and soft dough. Pick up the dough and transfer to a floured surface. With both hands, squeeze the dough through your fingers until the dough is so firm that you can't squeeze it through your fingers anymore, about 5 minutes. Continue to work the dough by stretching the dough horizontally with your fingers and hands. Then fold each side into the center, one over another, to form a long rectangle about 5 by 15 inches (13 by 38 cm), like a three-panel brochure. Turn the dough 90 degrees and repeat stretching the dough horizontally and folding, dusting with a little flour as necessary, until the dough is smooth and elastic, approximately five times. When you pull the dough apart it should stretch rather than break; then you will know you are ready.

Many older cookbooks call for kneading, including pushing, pulling, or hitting the dough during the process. I would advise against any of these, as they tear and shred the dough. Work the dough with care, moving it back and forth to develop gluten, but be aware of how your actions are affecting the dough.

Mixing Using an Electric Stand Mixer

The other method of mixing dough is by using an electric stand mixer. As stated in Chapter 1, a simple KitchenAid or other sturdy mixer with a dough hook will suffice. Bring the ingredients together in a rough form by mixing for 5 minutes on low speed (settings 2 to 3 if you have a KitchenAid). Finally, mix on medium speed for 5 minutes (settings 4 to 6 if you have a KitchenAid). Be careful not to overmix.

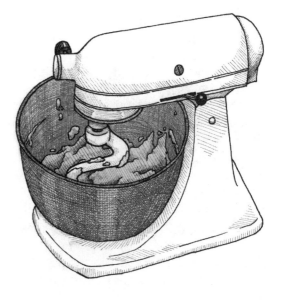

STEP 3: FIRST FERMENTATION

After mixing, place the dough in a warm area and allow the natural yeasts, in company with the other ingredients, to continue to ferment. You may think the bread is resting; however, the activity in the dough is increasing.

During this time, I would recommend rebuilding your starter with a feeding since you already have everything you need out.

Giving the bread time to rest improves the flavor and texture of the bread. The dough accumulates a volume of carbon dioxide gas, strong enough to expand the dough. During the rising, we see the bread grow before our eyes. The dough rises because the gluten network captures the carbon dioxide produced by the yeast, and the yeast in the starter feeds on the starches in the flour and continues to multiply. As a result, the carbon dioxide and other gases begin to give the dough volume and shape. The rising is needed to develop the gases, elasticity, flavor, texture, and volume that are so important to a good loaf of bread.

While you are waiting, a lot of things are happening in your dough, preparing it to become a superb loaf of bread.

To start the fermentation, lightly cover the dough. Some people lightly grease a bowl and put the dough in it, and then they cover it loosely with plastic wrap or a linen towel. Typically, I use a towel, which does the job nicely. Covering the dough prevents it from crusting and keeps it moist. After covering the dough, place it in a warm, draft-free spot. Where you let your dough rise depends on your own personal preference. Ideally, the temperature should be between 72 and 80°F (22 and 27°C). If you are in an especially drafty home, consider using a simple homemade proof box as described on page 20. Allow the dough to rise for 30 minutes to 3 hours, depending on the bread you are making.

The time frame gives a general idea of when the dough is ready for the next step. Just remember that it doesn't have to double in size, but it must be increasing in size. Again, you must learn to read your dough so that you can trust yourself to determine when that bread is ready for the next step.

STEP 4: PRE-SHAPING AND REST TIMES

After the first fermentation, we're ready to divide. Dust your clean work surface with flour. Cut the dough in half. With your hands, lightly form each piece into a round shape approximately 6 inches (15 cm) in diameter. This is called pre-shaping. Allow the dough 15 to 30 minutes to relax and rise. Cutting and handling the dough causes it to get a little bit tough, so you need to let the dough relax before the final forming.

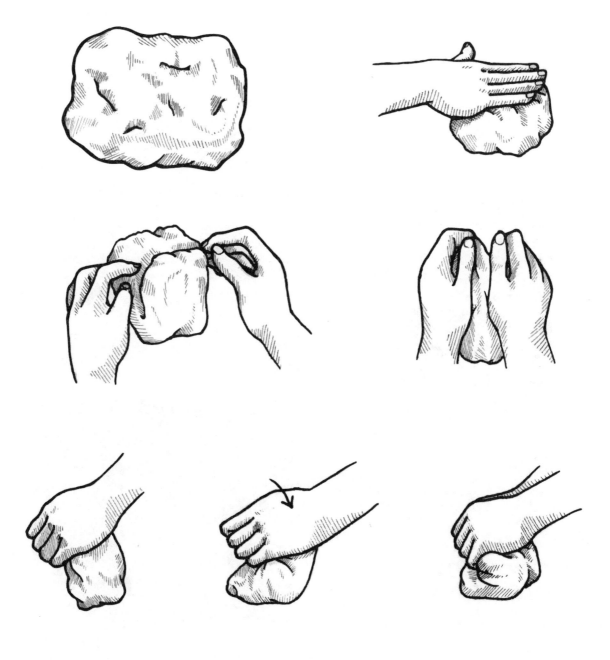

STEP 5: FINAL FORMING

For the final forming, use the palms of your hands to gently flatten the round pre-shaped dough. If the dough is sticking to the work surface, you can use a bit of flour. Be careful not to use too much flour or it may negatively affect the dough.

To form the round, fold one edge of the flattened, pre-shaped dough into the center. Make a quarter turn, fold the next edge to the center, and repeat this flattening, quarter turn, and repeat again. Put the dough on the work surface with the seam down and begin to form the round by cupping your hands around the dough. Using the base of your hands, keep rounding the dough and turning, using the table and your hands to tighten the dough until the round loaf is formed. Now we're ready for the next phase, the proofing.

1.

4.

Final Forming for Batard

Pat down in a long oval shape, with the long portion oriented vertically. Fold the top one-third of the dough toward you and pat down. Take the top two corners of the shape and bring them to the center of the dough. Pat out the air. Turn the dough 180 degrees, and repeat by folding the top one-third of the dough toward you and patting down. Take the top two corners of the shape and bring them into the center of the dough.

Pat out the air. Turn the seam side down, hold the dough with your fingers on the back side of the dough, and push the dough against the work surface with your thumbs, sealing and tightening the seam. Touch up the shape of the dough by gently rolling the oval until the desired shape is achieved.

1.

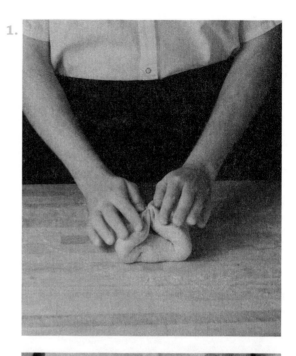

4.

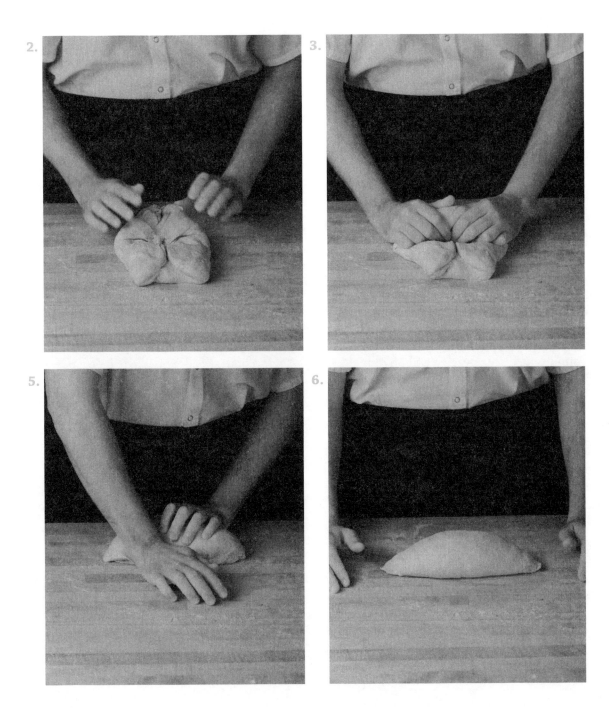

STEP 6: PROOFING OR FINAL FERMENTATION

Proofing, or the final rise, is done by placing the formed loaf onto a wooden board or oven peel that has been dusted with cornmeal. Proofing times for some doughs may be as little as 3 or fewer hours, while proofing time for the San Francisco sourdough will be 12 to 16 hours.

Dough follows a general, not strict, time frame. You must learn to read the loaf's progress so that you load the loaf into the oven at the best possible time. Depending on the climate you live in or the temperature of your house, doughs will rise differently.

In this final proof, the yeast has been feasting on carbohydrates while simultaneously releasing carbon dioxide and helping the flour's carbohydrates turn to alcohol. During the final proof, the yeast and bacteria reach the end of their food source.

However, yeast isn't the only force at work here. The decomposing enzymes in the flour also have a profound impact on the final loaf structure. For a while, the dough will continue to develop, aided by the effects of the yeast. However, if the loaf is left indefinitely, acids produced by the bacteria and enzyme activity will begin to ruin the loaf structure.

For example, if the loaf is baked too early or if it is not proofed long enough, it will be less flavorful and won't rise to its full size. Baking the loaf too late or overproofing will result in off flavors and a collapsed loaf.

So how do we know when it is time to bake? One of the first ways to judge is by looking at your loaf. Has it increased in volume by at least half? Now it is time to determine how much the dough has risen. Since we finished mixing the dough, it has been inflated with gas thanks in part to the gluten. During the final forming, we further develop the dough so that it will hold more gas and help maintain the shape of the loaf during baking.

One of the best ways to judge whether the loaf has finished rising is to press on the top of the loaf with a lightly floured index finger. If the imprint your finger leaves bounces back and almost disappears in a few seconds, the dough needs more time to ferment. The dough is still tight and needs more time to proof. It is a good practice to check regularly near the end of proofing time to see if the loaf is ready. When the loaf doesn't bounce back from your finger imprint, it is ready to bake.

STEP 7: BAKING
Preheating the Oven

During the time the loaves are proofing, you will want to preheat your oven. I recommend you preheat the oven, baking stone, and rebar pan for 3 hours. That sounds excessive, I know, but here's why: Our breads at Farm to Market have one hallmark that other bakers' breads might not—a deep browning in the loaf that permeates from the crust into the crumb, which is only achievable by baking in a hearth oven. To create a hearth oven at home, we use the baking stone. To be able to get the stone hot enough to brown the entire bread thoroughly, it must preheat for 3 hours. If you do not preheat the stone for 3 hours, only the top of the loaf will brown. That deep browning is called the Maillard (*my-YARD*) reaction, which is a chemical reaction resulting from the heat caramelizing and browning the crust. It's the same principle as what's behind the deep flavor you get when you let a pot roast brown in the oven. The Maillard reaction only happens with high, continuous heat. The caramelization produces a warming, mellow, delicious flavor that permeates the crumb of the loaf.

So, set the oven at 450°F (232°C). Let the oven preheat for 3 hours with your baking stone inside, along with your pan of rebar.

Now it is time for the baking. Once you place the loaf in the oven, an amazing physical, biological, and enzymatic change will occur. First comes what is known as oven jump. Oven jump could be considered the third rise. It expands the gases produced by yeast, expanding the dough, and increasing the loaf's volume.

While all of this is happening, the enzymes are very active on the surface of the loaf, converting starches into dextrin, which contributes to the coloration of the crust later in the baking. Meanwhile, as the loaf bakes, the crumb is being formed by the swollen wheat starch granules as they gelatinize. The gluten, which contributed to the firm structure before the loaf went into the oven, begins to stretch and expand. The starches in the loaf gelatinize when the temperature of the bread reaches about 200°F (90°C). As the loaf continues to bake, the crust still reacts to the heat in the oven. The crust will develop a rich brown color with the caramelization of the dough's sugar, creating a deep, rich flavor.

Once the loaf is placed in the oven, the heat will cause the dough to dry out, which will assist in creating the crust. We do not want the crust to form too early, because then it will not allow the gases to expand the loaf during the oven jump. So, it is important to steam the loaf at the beginning of the baking process, which keeps the dough moist, allowing the loaf to expand. After 10 minutes, open the oven to release the remaining steam to encourage the formation of the crust after the oven jump.

Two Ways to Create Steam

1. The Rebar Steam Method

Your first option to create steam for baking is to use a tray with the rebar steam method described in Chapter 1 (see page 19). Place the broiler pan with the rebar on the bottom shelf of the oven to preheat. The baking stone will be on the middle rack, above the broiler pan.

When the loaf is ready to bake, have ½ cup (120 g) water ready. To avoid steam burns, consider wearing a long-sleeved shirt and oven gloves. Score your loaf that is resting on the oven peel, open the oven door, and shift the loaf onto the stone. Immediately pour the water into the broiler pan with the hot rebar and shut the oven door right away. The steam will begin working on your loaf, giving it a good start to completing its work.

2. The Cloche Method

An alternative to pouring the water onto the hot rebar is to use the cloche method. With the cloche method, you will not need a broiler pan or rebar. Simply invert a stainless-steel bowl over the loaf to bake. Once the loaf is in the oven, immediately invert the bowl over top of the loaf, close the oven door, and bake the loaf. About halfway through the baking time, remove the bowl so the crust will continue to brown. The bowl will serve as a chamber to trap steam and moisture from the loaf.

STEP 8: COOLING

A quality loaf of bread is not at its best right out of the oven. As tempting as the smell is, as eager as you are to slather on the butter, bread needs time to cool to develop flavors. If sliced too early, the bread will collapse. The bread's finest aroma and flavor come when it has completely cooled. Sourdough bread does not come into its own until it has cooled for a few hours. This allows the flavors to settle and mingle.

In addition to developing the flavor of the bread, cooling allows the crust to stay firm and crisp by allowing evaporation of moisture. Once out of the oven, the bread continues to release steam and, as it cools, the crust becomes crisper.

Never try to hurry cooling bread, or put your bread in the refrigerator to cool. This will adversely affect the taste, texture, crumb, and crust.

Congratulations! You have completed the steps to making bread. The baking is done. The first loaf is finished. Now you can sit back and enjoy your bread, baked from a starter you made with the help of bacteria and yeast.

BREAD CARE

If the loaf is going to be eaten within 3 days, it is best kept on your countertop, unwrapped. The natural protection of a crusty exterior will preserve the soft interior crumb. Wrapping in plastic will create a soggy crust, which can be cured with a few minutes in a 400°F (205°C) oven. Do not store bread in the refrigerator, as it makes bread dry and stale. For longer storage, wrap the loaf and store in the freezer. When ready to enjoy, thaw at room temperature and reheat in a 400°F (205°C) oven for 3 to 5 minutes.

Remember that these are the basic steps to follow in any artisan bread you make. Paying close attention to this process will increase your chances of making a great loaf.

CHAPTER FOUR

SAN FRANCISCO
SOURDOUGH

MAKING YOUR FIRST SAN FRANCISCO SOURDOUGH LOAF

Even if baking bread is not your passion, bread itself should be a joy—a joy to watch as the mix of flour, water, and salt becomes a beautiful crusted loaf of bread. The more you bake and gain experience, the more your confidence will grow. Making bread does take practice. If the first loaf isn't quite right, a baker attuned to the dough will make changes necessary concerning the flour, the water, or the temperature of the day. Learning to read the dough enables you, after practice, to produce quality artisan bread.

We've talked about how bread from naturally fermented starter is good for the body. You saw how important it is to develop your starter and then continue to feed and nourish it, so it can help you make good bread. In this first recipe, you will learn how to make a loaf of bread from that starter.

I highly recommend that you start with the San Francisco Sourdough Boule to learn the basics and get the feel of this bread. After that, there are additional recipes to try in this chapter, especially before experimenting on your own. All the recipes use the San Francisco sourdough starter as their leavening agent. Most of the recipes call for the addition of ingredients that are best hand-mixed into the dough near the end of the mixing process. Be sure the ingredients are measured and prepared before adding them. Be sure to note whether any ingredient needs to be cooked before adding it to the dough.

Be careful not to mix the dough too hard when adding the extra ingredients. You want to be able to recognize these ingredients when the dough is sliced and not have them pulverized.

You will find using a sourdough starter, the final loaves will be characteristically tangy yet full-flavored, with a pleasingly airy crumb.

SAN FRANCISCO
SOURDOUGH BOULE

Makes 2 round loaves or boules

This first recipe is a simple loaf of San Francisco sourdough bread containing nothing more than flour, salt, water, and starter. Perfect it, learn the feel of the bread in your hands, and then—and only then—move to the recipes that include other ingredients. When you can make a great loaf of San Francisco sourdough bread, deliciously tangy with your natural starter, you'll know you're on the path to artisan baking.

SPONGE

½ cup plus 2 teaspoons (100 g) San Francisco Sourdough Starter (page 26)

⅔ cup plus 1 tablespoon (100 g) bread flour (page 21)

¼ cup (60 ml) water

DOUGH

3 ¼ cups (450 g) bread flour (page 21), plus more for dusting

1 ¼ cups (300 ml) water

2 teaspoons (11 g) salt

Sponge (use the entire sponge recipe made above)

Olive oil, for greasing

Cornmeal, for dusting

PREPARE THE SPONGE. In a large stainless-steel bowl, mix the starter, flour, and water together for about 4 minutes, using your hands until you have a dough mass. If using a stand mixer, mix on low (2 to 3 settings on a KitchenAid) for 4 minutes. It's important not to overmix the sponge. Cover with plastic wrap and let rise at room temperature until almost doubled in volume, 3 to 5 hours.

MIX THE DOUGH. To mix the dough by hand, add the flour, water, and salt to the sponge and mix with your hands or a dough scraper until you have a smooth and soft dough. Pick up the dough and transfer to a floured surface. With both hands, squeeze the dough through your fingers until the dough is so firm that you can't squeeze it through your fingers anymore, about 5 minutes. Continue to work the dough by stretching the dough horizontally with your fingers and hands. Then fold each side into the center, one over another, to form a long rectangle about 5 by 15 inches (13 by 38 cm), like a three-panel brochure.

Turn the dough 90 degrees and repeat stretching the dough horizontally and folding, dusting with a little flour as necessary, 5 times until the dough is smooth and elastic.

To mix using a stand mixer, transfer the sponge to the bowl of a stand mixer fitted with a dough hook and add the flour, water, and salt. Mix for 5 minutes on low speed (the 2 to 3 settings on a KitchenAid), scrape down the bowl and the dough hook, and then continue mixing for 5 more minutes on medium speed (the 4 to 6 settings on a KitchenAid), or until the dough is smooth and elastic.

FIRST FERMENTATION. Transfer the dough to a stainless-steel bowl that is lightly greased with olive oil. Cover with a kitchen towel and let rest for 30 minutes at room temperature.

PRE-SHAPE AND REST TIME. Transfer the dough to a floured surface. Divide in half with a metal dough scraper. Using your hands, gently pat and guide each half into a round shape about 6 inches (15 cm) in diameter. Cover with a kitchen towel and let rest for another 15 minutes before the final forming.

FINAL FORMING. Dust your hands with flour. Use a dough scraper to lift the dough rounds off the floured surface to make sure they're not sticky. (If they are, gently brush your floured hands over the sticky places.) With your hands, pick up an edge of the dough and pull it to the center of the dough round. Make a quarter turn, fold the next edge to the center, and repeat this flattening, quarter turn, and repeat again. Then flip the dough over so the seams are facing down on the work surface. Cupping your hands, gently round the dough with pressure against the work surface. Repeat with the second dough round. Each boule should be about 6 inches (15 cm) in diameter.

FINAL FERMENTATION. Place the formed boules on a cornmeal-covered surface. Cover each boule with loose plastic wrap or a kitchen towel and let proof for 12 to 16 hours at room temperature, above 72°F (22°C).

To prepare the oven for cloche baking, place 1 oven rack on the lower third of the oven. Place a baking stone on the oven rack. Remove the second oven rack. When placing the boule in the oven, quickly invert a stainless-steel bowl over the loaf, creating a loose seal with the baking stone, and close the oven door. Remove the stainless-steel bowl after 10 minutes of baking to release the steam.

To prepare the oven for rebar steam baking, place an oven rack on the lowest rung of the oven. Arrange 10 small rebar in a single row along the bottom of a broiler pan; place the broiler pan on the lower oven rack. Arrange the second oven rack just above the broiler pan. Place a baking stone on the second, higher oven rack. After you put the loaf in the oven, pour ½ cup (120 ml) room-temperature water into the prepared broiler pan. Be careful of the hot steam. Quickly close the oven door.

BAKE. After preparing the oven for either method of steam, preheat the oven to 450°F (232°C) for 3 hours. Lightly coat a wooden peel with cornmeal. Gently place 1 boule on the prepared peel. With a bread lame or razor blade slanted at a 45-degree angle, make 3 horizontal and 3 vertical slashes (like a tic-tac-toe game), ⅛ to ¼ inch (3 to 6 mm) deep, across the top of each boule. Slide the boule off the oven peel onto the baking stone in the oven. (If using the rebar method, pour water into the broiler pan. If using the cloche method, place a stainless-steel bowl over the boule immediately after sliding the boule into the oven and remove the bowl after 10 minutes, as described above.) Total loaf bake time is 30 to 35 minutes, until the boule has turned a golden brown and sounds hollow when tapped on the bottom of the loaf in the center.

COOL ON A COOLING RACK. Repeat the baking process with the second loaf after allowing the oven and baking stone to come back to temperature, about 15 minutes. If the loaf is going to be eaten within 3 days, it is best kept on your countertop, unwrapped. The natural protection of the crusty exterior will preserve the soft interior crumb. For longer storage, wrap the loaf and store in the freezer. When ready to enjoy, thaw at room temperature and reheat in a 400°F (205°C) oven for 3 to 5 minutes.

CHILE-CHEESE
SOURDOUGH BOULE
Makes 2 round loaves or boules

Chile-cheese has been a very popular sourdough variation at Farm to Market Bread Company for many years. Made in the fall, the bread celebrates the changing seasons and the start of football. To get the best flavor and texture, the dough needs to rest for 12 to 16 hours before baking, so count on a two-day bread-making process. You will bake one round loaf at a time on your baking stone. Because the cheese can ooze out of this loaf and burn on your baking stone, you line the peel with a sheet of parchment paper and transfer the loaf and paper to the baking stone. Problem solved! The parchment paper might get a little scorched on the ends, but it will not burn. This colorful, tangy bread makes an unforgettable grilled cheese sandwich or patty melt. If you wish, you can freeze the second loaf for up to 3 months.

SPONGE

½ cup (80 g) San Francisco Sourdough Starter (page 26)

½ cup plus 1 tablespoon and 1 teaspoon (80 g) bread flour (page 21)

3 tablespoons (45 ml) water, 78–82°F (26–28°C)

DOUGH

2 ¾ cups plus 1 teaspoon (380 g) bread flour (page 21), plus more for dusting

1 cup (240 ml) water, 78–82°F (26–28°C)

2 teaspoons (11 g) salt

1 ¾ cups (195 g) cheddar cheese cut into ½-inch (1 cm) cubes

⅓ cup (45 g) stemmed, seeded, and finely chopped fresh chile peppers (your choice of type)

Olive oil, for greasing

Cornmeal, for dusting

PREPARE THE SPONGE. In a large stainless-steel bowl, mix the starter, flour, and water together for about 4 minutes, using your hands until you have a dough mass. If using a stand mixer, mix on low (2 to 3 settings on a KitchenAid) for 4 minutes. It's important not to overmix the sponge. Cover with plastic wrap and let rise at room temperature until almost doubled in volume, 3 to 5 hours.

MIX THE DOUGH. To mix by hand, add the flour, water, and salt to the sponge and mix with your hands or a dough scraper until you have a smooth and soft dough. Pick up the dough and transfer to a floured surface. With both hands, squeeze the dough through your fingers until the dough is so firm that you can't squeeze it through your fingers anymore, about 5 minutes. Continue to work the dough by stretching the dough horizontally with your fingers and hands. Then fold each side into the center, one over another, to form a long rectangle about 5 by 15 inches (13 by 38 cm), like a three-panel brochure. Turn the dough 90 degrees and repeat stretching the dough horizontally and folding, dusting with a little flour as necessary, until the dough is smooth and elastic, approximately 5 times.

To mix using a stand mixer, transfer the sponge to the bowl of a stand mixer fitted with a dough hook and add the flour, water, and salt. Mix for 5 minutes on low speed (the 2 to 3 settings on a KitchenAid), scrape down the bowl and the dough hook, and then continue mixing for 5 minutes on medium speed (the 4 to 6 settings on a KitchenAid), or until the dough is smooth and elastic.

After the dough has been mixed, place it on a floured surface and pat down by hand, spreading the dough out. Scatter the cheese and chiles on top of the dough and fold the sides of the dough over, essentially enclosing the cheese and chiles inside the dough. Then with a metal dough scraper, randomly chop the dough. By hand, bring the dough back together by folding and patting until you have a smooth dough studded with all the cheese and chiles.

FIRST FERMENTATION. Transfer the dough to a stainless-steel bowl lightly greased with olive oil. Cover with a kitchen towel and let rest for 30 minutes at room temperature.

PRE-SHAPE AND REST TIME. Transfer the dough to a floured surface. Divide in half with a metal dough scraper. Using your hands, gently pat and guide each half into a round shape about 6 inches (15 cm) in diameter. Cover with a kitchen towel and let rest for another 15 minutes before the final forming.

FINAL FORMING. Dust your hands with flour. Use a dough scraper to lift the dough rounds off the floured surface to make sure they're not sticky. (If they are, gently brush your floured hands over the sticky places.) With your hands, pick up an edge of the dough and pull it to the center of the dough round. Make a quarter turn, fold the next edge to the center, and repeat this flattening, quarter turn, and repeat again. Then flip the dough over so the seams are facing down on the work surface. Cupping your hands, gently round the dough with pressure against the work surface. Repeat with the second dough round. Each boule should be about 6 inches (15 cm) in diameter.

FINAL FERMENTATION. Place the formed boules on a cornmeal-covered surface. Cover each boule with loose plastic wrap or a kitchen towel and let proof for 12 to 16 hours at room temperature, above 72° F (22°C).

To prepare the oven for cloche baking, place 1 oven rack on the lower third of the oven. Place a baking stone on the oven rack.

Remove the second oven rack. When placing the boule in the oven, quickly invert a stainless-steel bowl over the loaf, creating a loose seal with the baking stone, and close the oven door. Remove the stainless-steel bowl after 10 minutes of baking to release the steam.

To prepare the oven for rebar steam baking, place an oven rack on the lowest rung of the oven. Arrange 10 small rebar in a single row along the bottom of a broiler pan; place the broiler pan on the lower oven rack. Arrange the second oven rack just above the broiler pan. Place a baking stone on the second, higher oven rack. After you put the loaf in the oven, pour ½ cup (120 ml) room-temperature water into the prepared broiler pan. Be careful of the hot steam. Quickly close the oven door.

BAKE. After preparing the oven for either method of steam, preheat the oven to 450°F (232°C) for 3 hours. Lightly coat a wooden peel with cornmeal. Gently place one boule on the prepared peel. With a bread lame or razor blade slanted at a 45-degree angle, make 3 horizontal and 3 vertical slashes (like a tic-tac-toe game), ⅛ to ¼ inch (3 to 6 mm) deep, across the top of each boule. Slide the boule off the oven peel onto the baking stone in the oven. (If using the rebar method, pour water into the broiler pan. If using the cloche method, place a stainless-steel bowl over the boule immediately after sliding the boule into the oven and remove the bowl after 10 minutes, as described above.) Total loaf bake time is 30 to 35 minutes, until the boule has turned a golden brown and sounds hollow when tapped on the bottom of the loaf in the center.

COOL ON A COOLING RACK. Repeat the baking process with the second loaf after allowing the oven and baking stone to come back to temperature, about 15 minutes. If the loaf is going to be eaten within 3 days, it is best kept on your countertop, unwrapped. The natural protection of the crusty exterior will preserve the soft interior crumb. For longer storage, wrap the loaf and store in the freezer. When ready to enjoy, thaw at room temperature and reheat in a 400°F (205°C) oven for 3 to 5 minutes.

CRANBERRY-ORANGE
SOURDOUGH BOULE

Makes 2 round loaves or boules

Cranberry and orange go well together in festive holiday dishes but also in breads. The combination of the candied orange peel as well as the fresh orange zest with the sourdough creates a unique flavor; it gives the sourdough an almost sweet taste, with the tang of the sour lingering in the background. The cranberries add little pops of color.

SPONGE

½ cup (80 g) San Francisco Sourdough Starter (page 26)

½ cup plus 1 tablespoon and 1 teaspoon (80 g) bread flour (page 21)

3 tablespoons (45 ml) water, 78–82°F (26–28°C)

DOUGH

2 ¾ cups plus 1 teaspoon (380 g) bread flour (page 21), plus more for dusting

1 cup (240 ml) water, 78–82°F (26–28°C)

2 teaspoons (11 g) salt

1 cup (125 g) dried cranberries

1 cup (100 g) candied orange peel, cut into ½-inch (1 cm) pieces

1 tablespoon (5 g) finely grated orange zest

Olive oil, for greasing

Cornmeal, for dusting

PREPARE THE SPONGE. In a large stainless-steel bowl, mix the starter, flour, and water together for about 4 minutes, using your hands until you have a dough mass. If using a stand mixer, mix on low (2 to 3 settings on a KitchenAid) for 4 minutes. It's important not to overmix the sponge. Cover with plastic wrap and let rise at room temperature until almost doubled in volume, 3 to 5 hours.

MIX THE DOUGH. To mix by hand, add the flour, water, and salt to the sponge and mix with your hands or a dough scraper until you have a smooth and soft dough. Pick up the dough and transfer to a floured surface. With both hands, squeeze the dough through your fingers until the dough is so firm that you can't squeeze it through your fingers anymore, about 5 minutes. Continue to work the dough by stretching the dough horizontally with your fingers and hands. Then fold each side into the center, one over another, to form a long rectangle about 5 by 15 inches (13 by 38 cm), like a three-panel brochure. Turn the dough 90 degrees and repeat stretching the dough horizontally and folding, dusting with a little flour as necessary, until the dough is smooth and elastic, approximately 5 times.

To mix using a stand mixer, transfer the sponge to the bowl of a stand mixer fitted with a dough hook and add the flour, water, and salt. Mix for 5 minutes on low speed (the 2 to 3 settings on a KitchenAid), scrape down the bowl and the dough hook, and then continue mixing for 5 minutes on medium speed (the 4 to 6 settings on a KitchenAid), or until the dough is smooth and elastic.

After the dough has been mixed, place it on a floured surface and pat down by hand, spreading the dough out. Scatter the cranberries, orange peel, and orange zest on top of the dough and fold the sides of the dough over, essentially enclosing the cranberries, peel, and zest inside the dough. Then with a metal dough scraper, randomly chop the dough. By hand, bring the dough back together by folding and patting until you have a smooth dough studded with all the cranberries and orange peel.

FIRST FERMENTATION. Transfer the dough to a stainless-steel bowl lightly greased with olive oil. Cover with a kitchen towel and let rest for 30 minutes at room temperature.

PRE-SHAPE AND REST TIME. Transfer the dough to a floured surface. Divide in half with a metal dough scraper. Using your hands, gently pat and guide each half into a round shape about 6 inches (15 cm) in diameter. Cover with a kitchen towel and let rest for another 15 minutes before the final forming.

FINAL FORMING. Dust your hands with flour. Use a dough scraper to lift the dough rounds off the floured surface to make sure they're not sticky. (If they are, gently brush your floured hands over the sticky places.) With your hands, pick up an edge of the dough and pull it to the center of the dough round. Make a quarter turn, fold the next edge to the center, and repeat this flattening, quarter turn, and repeat again. Then flip the dough over so the seams are facing down on the work surface. Cupping your hands, gently round the dough with pressure against the work surface. Repeat with the second dough round. Each boule should be about 6 inches (15 cm) in diameter.

FINAL FERMENTATION. Place the formed boules on a cornmeal-covered surface. Cover each boule with loose plastic wrap or a kitchen towel and let proof for 12 to 16 hours at room temperature, above 72°F (22°C).

To prepare the oven for cloche baking, place 1 oven rack on the lower third of the oven. Place a baking stone on the oven rack. Remove the second oven rack. When placing the boule in the oven, quickly invert a stainless-steel bowl over the loaf, creating a loose seal with the baking stone, and close the oven door. Remove the bowl after 10 minutes of baking to release the steam.

(Continued on page 68)

CRANBERRY-ORANGE
SOURDOUGH BOULE

To prepare the oven for rebar steam baking, place an oven rack on the lowest rung of the oven. Arrange 10 small rebar in a single row along the bottom of a broiler pan; place the broiler pan on the lower oven rack. Arrange the second oven rack just above the broiler pan. Place a baking stone on the second, higher oven rack. After you put the loaf in the oven, pour ½ cup (120 ml) room-temperature water into the prepared broiler pan. Be careful of the hot steam. Quickly close the oven door.

BAKE. After preparing the oven for either method of steam, preheat the oven to 450°F (232°C) for 3 hours. Lightly coat a wooden peel with cornmeal. Gently place 1 boule on the prepared peel. With a bread lame or razor blade slanted at a 45-degree angle, make 3 horizontal and 3 vertical slashes (like a tic-tac-toe game), ⅛ to ¼ inch (3 to 6 mm) deep, across the top of each boule. Slide the boule off the oven peel onto the baking stone in the oven.

(If using the rebar method, pour water into the broiler pan. If using the cloche method, place a stainless-steel bowl over the boule immediately after sliding the boule into the oven and remove the bowl after 10 minutes, as described above.) Total loaf bake time is 30 to 35 minutes, until the boule has turned a golden brown and sounds hollow when tapped on the bottom of the loaf in the center.

COOL ON A COOLING RACK. Repeat the baking process with the second loaf after allowing the oven and baking stone to come back to temperature, about 15 minutes. If the loaf is going to be eaten within 3 days, it is best kept on your countertop, unwrapped. The natural protection of the crusty exterior will preserve the soft interior crumb. For longer storage, wrap the loaf and store in the freezer. When ready to enjoy, thaw at room temperature and reheat in a 400°F (205°C) oven for 3 to 5 minutes.

ARTICHOKE-PARMESAN
SOURDOUGH BOULE

Makes 2 round loaves or boules

This is an interesting bread, guaranteed to keep people guessing as to what the ingredients are in such a delicious loaf. I suggest you use bottled as opposed to canned artichokes to develop a better flavor.

SPONGE

½ cup (80 g) San Francisco Sourdough Starter (page 26)

½ cup plus 1 tablespoon and 1 teaspoon (80 g) bread flour (page 21)

3 tablespoons (45 ml) water, 78–82°F (26–28°C)

DOUGH

2 ¾ cups plus 1 teaspoon (380 g) bread flour (page 21), plus more for dusting

1 cup (240 ml) water, 78–82°F (26–28°C)

2 teaspoons (11 g) salt

1 cup (100 g) grated Parmesan cheese

½ cup plus 1 tablespoon (100 g) bottled artichoke hearts, drained, patted dry, and chopped into ½-inch (1 cm) pieces

Olive oil, for greasing

Cornmeal, for dusting

PREPARE THE SPONGE. In a large stainless-steel bowl, mix the starter, flour, and water together for about 4 minutes, using your hands until you have a dough mass. If using a stand mixer, mix on low (2 to 3 settings on a KitchenAid) for 4 minutes. It's important not to overmix the sponge. Cover with plastic wrap and let rise at room temperature until almost doubled in volume, 3 to 5 hours.

MIX THE DOUGH. To mix by hand, add the flour, water, and salt to the sponge and mix with your hands or a dough scraper until you have a smooth and soft dough. Pick up the dough and transfer to a floured surface. With both hands, squeeze the dough through your fingers until the dough is so firm that you can't squeeze it through your fingers anymore, about 5 minutes. Continue to work the dough by stretching the dough horizontally with your fingers and hands. Then fold each side into the center, one over another, to form a long rectangle about 5 by 15 inches (13 by 38 cm), like a three-panel brochure. Turn the dough 90 degrees and repeat stretching the dough horizontally and folding, dusting with a little flour as necessary, until the dough is smooth and elastic, approximately 5 times.

To mix using a stand mixer, transfer the sponge to the bowl of a stand mixer fitted with a dough hook and add the flour, water, and salt. Mix for 5 minutes on low speed (the 2 to 3 settings on a KitchenAid), scrape down the bowl and the dough hook, and then continue mixing for 5 minutes on medium speed (4 to 6 settings on a KitchenAid), or until the dough is smooth and elastic.

After the dough has been mixed, place it on a floured surface and pat down by hand, spreading the dough out. Scatter the cheese and artichokes on top of the dough and fold the sides of the dough over, essentially enclosing the cheese and artichokes inside the dough. Then with a metal dough scraper, randomly chop the dough. By hand, bring the dough back together by folding and patting until you have a smooth dough studded with all the cheese and artichokes.

FIRST FERMENTATION. Transfer the dough to a stainless-steel bowl lightly greased with olive oil. Cover with a kitchen towel and let rest for 30 minutes at room temperature.

PRE-SHAPE AND REST TIME. Transfer the dough to a floured surface. Divide in half with a metal dough scraper. Using your hands, gently pat and guide each half into a round shape about 6 inches (15 cm) in diameter. Cover with a kitchen towel and let rest for another 15 minutes before the final forming.

FINAL FORMING. Dust your hands with flour. Use a dough scraper to lift the dough rounds off the floured surface to make sure they're not sticky. (If they are, gently brush your floured hands over the sticky places.) With your hands, pick up an edge of the dough and pull it to the center of the dough round. Make a quarter turn, fold the next edge to the center, and repeat this flattening, quarter turn, and repeat again. Then flip the dough over so the seams are facing down on the work surface. Cupping your hands, gently round the dough with pressure against the work surface. Repeat with the second dough boule. Each boule should be about 6 inches (15 cm) in diameter.

FINAL FERMENTATION. Place the formed boules on a cornmeal-covered surface. Cover each boule with loose plastic wrap or a kitchen towel and let proof for 12 to 16 hours at room temperature, above 72°F (22°C).

To prepare the oven for cloche baking, place 1 oven rack on the lower third of the oven. Place a baking stone on the oven rack. Remove the second oven rack. When placing the boule in the oven, quickly invert a stainless-steel bowl over the loaf, creating a loose seal with the baking stone, and close the oven door. Remove the bowl after 10 minutes of baking to release the steam.

To prepare the oven for rebar steam baking, place an oven rack on the lowest rung of the oven. Arrange 10 small rebar in a single row along the bottom of a broiler pan; place the broiler pan on the lower oven rack. Arrange the second oven rack just above the broiler pan. Place a baking stone on the second, higher oven rack. After you put the loaf in the oven, pour ½ cup (120 ml) room-temperature water into the prepared broiler pan. Be careful of the hot steam. Quickly close the oven door.

BAKE. After preparing the oven for either method of steam, preheat the oven to 450°F (232°C) for 3 hours. Lightly coat a wooden peel with cornmeal. Gently place 1 boule on the prepared peel. With a bread lame or razor blade slanted at a 45-degree angle, make 3 horizontal and 3 vertical slashes (like a tic-tac-toe game), ⅛ to ¼ inch (3 to 6 mm) deep, across the top of each boule. Slide the boule off the oven peel onto the baking stone in the oven. (If using the rebar method, pour water into the broiler pan. If using the cloche method, place a stainless-steel bowl over the boule immediately after sliding the boule into the oven and remove the bowl after 10 minutes, as described above.) Total loaf bake time is 30 to 35 minutes, until the boule has turned a golden brown and sounds hollow when tapped on the bottom of the loaf in the center.

COOL ON A COOLING RACK. Repeat the baking process with the second loaf after allowing the oven and baking stone to come back to temperature, about 15 minutes. If the loaf is going to be eaten within 3 days, it is best kept on your countertop, unwrapped. The natural protection of the crusty exterior will preserve the soft interior crumb. For longer storage, wrap the loaf and store in the freezer. When ready to enjoy, thaw at room temperature and reheat in a 400°F (205°C) oven for 3 to 5 minutes.

PUMPKIN-SUNFLOWER SEED
SOURDOUGH BOULE

Makes 2 round loaves or boules

This bread has an interesting crunch from both pumpkin and sunflower seed kernels. Pumpkin seed kernels, known as pepitas, are olive green in color, buttery in texture, and nutty in flavor. They're also full of protein, antioxidants, healthy fats, and other good things. Light-brown sunflower kernels are likewise full of minerals, antioxidants, and vitamins.

SPONGE

- ½ cup (80 g) San Francisco Sourdough Starter (page 26)
- ½ cup plus 1 tablespoon and 1 teaspoon (80 g) bread flour (page 21)
- 3 tablespoons (45 ml) water, 78–82°F (26–28°C)

DOUGH

- 2 ¾ cups plus 1 teaspoon (380 g) bread flour (page 21), plus more for dusting
- 1 cup (240 ml) water, 78–82°F (26–28°C)
- 2 teaspoons (11 g) salt
- ¾ cup plus 1 tablespoon (120 g) roasted sunflower seed kernels
- ½ cup (80 g) roasted pumpkin seed kernels (pepitas)
- Olive oil, for greasing
- Cornmeal, for dusting

PREPARE THE SPONGE. In a large stainless-steel bowl, mix the starter, flour, and water together for about 4 minutes, using your hands until you have a dough mass. If using a stand mixer, mix on low (2 to 3 settings on a KitchenAid) for 4 minutes. It's important not to overmix the sponge. Cover with plastic wrap and let rise at room temperature until almost doubled in volume, 3 to 5 hours.

MIX THE DOUGH. To mix by hand, add the flour, water, salt, sunflower seed kernels, and pumpkin seed kernels to the sponge and mix with your hands or a dough scraper until you have a smooth and soft dough. Pick up the dough and transfer to a floured surface. With both hands, squeeze the dough through your fingers until the dough is so firm that you can't squeeze it through your fingers anymore, about 5 minutes. Continue to work the dough by stretching the dough horizontally with your fingers and hands. Then fold each side into the center, one over another, to form a long rectangle about 5 by 15 inches (13 by 38 cm), like a three-panel brochure. Turn the dough 90 degrees and repeat stretching the dough horizontally and folding, dusting with a little flour as necessary, until the dough is smooth and elastic, approximately 5 times.

To mix using a stand mixer, transfer the sponge to the bowl of a stand mixer fitted with a dough hook and add the flour, water, salt, sunflower seed kernels, and pumpkin seed kernels. Mix for 5 minutes on low speed (the 2 to 3 settings on a KitchenAid), scrape down the bowl and the dough hook, and then continue mixing for 5 minutes on medium speed (the 4 to 6 settings on a KitchenAid), or until the dough is smooth and elastic.

FIRST FERMENTATION. Transfer the dough to a stainless-steel bowl lightly greased with olive oil. Cover with a kitchen towel and let rest for 30 minutes at room temperature.

PRE-SHAPE AND REST TIME. Transfer the dough to a floured surface. Divide in half with a metal dough scraper. Using your hands, gently pat and guide each half into a round shape about 6 inches (15cm) in diameter. Cover with a kitchen towel and let rest for another 15 minutes before the final forming.

FINAL FORMING. Dust your hands with flour. Use a dough scraper to lift the dough rounds off the floured surface to make sure they're not sticky. (If they are, gently brush your floured hands over the sticky places.)

With your hands, pick up an edge of the dough and pull it to the center of the dough round. Make a quarter turn, fold the next edge to the center, and repeat this flattening, quarter turn, and repeat again. Then flip the dough over so the seams are facing down on the work surface. Cupping your hands, gently round the dough with pressure against the work surface. Repeat with the second dough round. Each boule should be about 6 inches (15 cm) in diameter.

FINAL FERMENTATION. Place the formed boules on a cornmeal-covered surface. Cover each boule with loose plastic wrap or a kitchen towel and let proof for 12 to 16 hours at room temperature, above 72°F (22°C).

To prepare the oven for rebar steam baking, place an oven rack on the lowest rung of the oven. Arrange 10 small rebar in a single row along the bottom of a broiler pan; place the broiler pan on the lower oven rack. Arrange the second oven rack just above the broiler pan. Place a baking stone on the second, higher oven rack. After you put the loaf in the oven, pour ½ cup (120 ml) room-temperature water into the prepared broiler pan. Be careful of the hot steam. Quickly close the oven door.

To prepare the oven for cloche baking, place 1 oven rack on the lower third of the oven. Place a baking stone on the oven rack. Remove the second oven rack. When placing the boule in the oven, quickly invert

a stainless-steel bowl over the loaf, creating a loose seal with the baking stone, and close the oven door. Remove the bowl after 10 minutes of baking to release the steam.

BAKE. After preparing the oven for either method of steam, preheat the oven to 450°F (232°C) for 3 hours. Lightly coat a wooden peel with cornmeal. Gently place 1 boule on the prepared peel. With a bread lame or razor blade slanted at a 45-degree angle, make 3 horizontal and 3 vertical slashes (like a tic-tac-toe game), ⅛ to ¼ inch (3 to 6 cm) deep, across the top of each boule. Slide the boule off the oven peel onto the baking stone in the oven. (If using the rebar method, pour water into the broiler pan. If using the cloche method, place a stainless-steel bowl over the boule immediately after sliding the boule into the oven and remove the bowl after 10 minutes, as described above.) Total loaf bake time is 30 to 35 minutes, until the boule has turned a golden brown and sounds hollow when tapped on the bottom of the loaf in the center.

COOL ON A COOLING RACK. Repeat the baking process with the second loaf after allowing the oven and baking stone to come back to temperature, about 15 minutes. If the loaf is going to be eaten within 3 days, it is best kept on your countertop, unwrapped. The natural protection of the crusty exterior will preserve the soft interior crumb. For longer storage, wrap the loaf and store in the freezer. When ready to enjoy, thaw at room temperature and reheat in a 400°F (205°C) oven for 3 to 5 minutes.

POTATO-ONION
SOURDOUGH BOULE
Makes 2 round loaves or boules

Potatoes. Onions. Sourdough. Who could ask for a heartier loaf, a great accompaniment to soups? If you like, bake the potato and sauté the onions while the sponge is rising. Again, allow 2 days for making this bread, as it needs 12 to 16 hours to proof and develop its great sourdough flavor.

SPONGE

½ cup (80 g) San Francisco Sourdough Starter (page 26)

½ cup plus 1 tablespoon and 1 teaspoon (80 g) bread flour (page 21)

3 tablespoons (45 ml) water, 78–82°F (26–28°C)

DOUGH

2 ¾ cups plus 1 teaspoon (380 g) bread flour (page 21), plus more for dusting

1 cup (240 ml) water, 78–82°F (26–28°C)

2 teaspoons (11 g) salt

1 teaspoon (0.7 g) fresh rosemary leaves

¾ cup (150 g) peeled and chopped baked potato, cooled

⅓ cup (50 g) chopped white, red, or yellow onions sautéed in 1 tablespoon (15 ml) olive oil until golden brown

Olive oil, for greasing

Cornmeal, for dusting

PREPARE THE SPONGE. In a large stainless-steel bowl, mix the starter, flour, and water together for about 4 minutes, using your hands until you have a dough mass. If using a stand mixer, mix on low (2 to 3 settings on a KitchenAid) for 4 minutes. It's important not to overmix the sponge. Cover with plastic wrap and let rise at room temperature until almost doubled in volume, 3 to 5 hours.

MIX THE DOUGH. To mix by hand, add the flour, water, salt, and rosemary to the sponge and mix with your hands or a dough scraper until you have a smooth and soft dough. Pick up the dough and transfer to a floured surface. With both hands, squeeze the dough through your fingers until the dough is so firm that you can't squeeze it through your fingers anymore, about 5 minutes. Continue to work the dough by stretching the dough horizontally with your fingers and hands. Then fold each side into the center, one over another, to form a long rectangle about 5 by 15 inches (13 by 38 cm), like a three-panel brochure. Turn the dough 90 degrees and repeat stretching the dough horizontally and folding, dusting with a little flour as necessary, until the dough is smooth and elastic, approximately 5 times.

To mix using a stand mixer, transfer the sponge to the bowl of a stand mixer fitted with a dough hook and add the flour, water, and salt. Mix for 5 minutes on low speed (the 2 to 3 settings on a KitchenAid), scrape down the bowl and the dough hook, and then continue mixing for 5 minutes on medium speed (the 4 to 6 settings on a KitchenAid), or until the dough is smooth and elastic.

After the dough has been mixed, place it on a floured surface and pat down by hand, spreading the dough out. Scatter the potato and onions on top of the dough and fold the sides of the dough over, essentially enclosing the potato and onions inside the dough. Then with a metal dough scraper, randomly chop the dough. By hand, bring the dough back together by folding and patting until you have a smooth dough studded with all the potato and onions.

FIRST FERMENTATION. Transfer the dough to a stainless-steel bowl lightly greased with olive oil. Cover with a kitchen towel and let rest for 30 minutes at room temperature, above 72°F (22°C).

PRE-SHAPE AND REST TIME.
Transfer the dough to a floured surface. Divide in half with a metal dough scraper.

Using your hands, gently pat and guide each half into a round shape about 6 inches (15 cm) in diameter. Cover with a kitchen towel and let rest for another 15 minutes before the final forming.

FINAL FORMING. Dust your hands with flour. Use a dough scraper to lift the dough rounds off the floured surface to make sure they're not sticky. (If they are, gently brush your floured hands over the sticky places.) With your hands, pick up an edge of the dough and pull it to the center of the dough round. Make a quarter turn, fold the next edge to the center, and repeat this flattening, quarter turn, and repeat again. Then flip the dough over so the seams are facing down on the work surface. Cupping your hands, gently round the dough with pressure against the work surface. Repeat with the second dough round. Each boule should be about 6 inches (15 cm) in diameter.

FINAL FERMENTATION. Place the formed boules on a cornmeal-covered surface. Cover each boule with loose plastic wrap or a kitchen towel and let proof for 12 to 16 hours at room temperature, above 72°F (22°C).

To prepare the oven for rebar steam baking, place an oven rack on the lowest rung of the oven. Arrange 10 small rebar in a single row along the bottom of a broiler pan; place the broiler pan on the lower oven rack. Arrange the second oven rack just above the broiler pan. Place a baking stone on the second, higher oven rack. After you put the loaf in the oven, pour ½ cup (120 ml) room-temperature water into the prepared broiler pan. Be careful of the hot steam. Quickly close the oven door.

To prepare the oven for cloche baking, place 1 oven rack on the lower third of the oven. Place a baking stone on the oven rack. Remove the second oven rack. When placing the boule in the oven, quickly invert a stainless-steel bowl over the loaf, creating a loose seal with the baking stone, and close the oven door. Remove the bowl after 10 minutes of baking to release the steam.

BAKE. After preparing the oven for either method of steam, preheat the oven to 450°F (232°C) for 3 hours. Lightly coat a wooden peel with cornmeal. Gently place 1 boule on the prepared peel. With a bread lame or razor blade slanted at a 45-degree angle, make 3 horizontal and 3 vertical slashes (like a tic-tac-toe game), ⅛ to ¼ inch (3 to 6 mm) deep, across the top of each boule.

Slide the boule off the oven peel onto the baking stone in the oven. (If using the rebar method, pour water into the broiler pan. If using the cloche method, place a stainless-steel bowl over the boule immediately after sliding the boule into the oven and remove the bowl after 10 minutes, as described above.) Total loaf bake time is 30 to 35 minutes, until the boule has turned a golden brown and sounds hollow when tapped on the bottom of the loaf in the center.

COOL ON A COOLING RACK. Repeat the baking process with the second loaf after allowing the oven and baking stone to come back to temperature, about 15 minutes. If the loaf is going to be eaten within 3 days, it is best kept on your countertop, unwrapped. The natural protection of the crusty exterior will preserve the soft interior crumb. For longer storage, wrap the loaf and store in the freezer. When ready to enjoy, thaw at room temperature and reheat in a 400°F (205°C) oven for 3 to 5 minutes.

CHAPTER FIVE

LEVAIN, THE FRENCH
NATURAL LEAVEN

BAKING WITH LEVAIN allows the baker to work with a starter that is more fluid than the stiff San Francisco sourdough starter. It tends to rise quicker. Before long, you will get to know this starter as well as you did the San Francisco sourdough.

To achieve the best flavor and texture in this bread, you will use a combination of flours, but mainly higher-protein bread flour. For my recommended flours, see page 21.

French Farm (page 80), a wonderfully rustic type of loaf, is the basic bread made with levain. Once you have the basics of levain—and you are feeding it regularly—you can move on to other types of bread that use this starter, such as Kalamata (page 83), Sun-Dried Tomato (page 89), and Raisin-Walnut (page 93).

This is just the beginning of what you can do with levain. And one of the best things is, if you make a commitment to levain, the starter is always there waiting for you to form it into delicious loaves of healthy bread.

FRENCH FARM

Makes 2 round loaves or boules

The French have been baking this bread in village ovens for centuries, the tops crosshatched with the individual marks of each family so that they would know which loaf was theirs when it came out of the oven. This French Farm Boule predates what many people think is the classic French bread—the long and thin baguette, which was first made about 1920. This round loaf lends itself to flavor additions, as you'll see in subsequent recipes. But it is delicious on its own. It has the crisp, dark, blistered crust and airy interior of the best French bread. And you have the satisfaction of having made it all yourself. Unlike the sourdough breads, you don't need to start with a sponge. You just mix the starter right in the dough. To get the best flavor and texture, you need to use a mix of flours. See page 21 for those I recommend. You will also need two proofing baskets. If you start in the morning, you can have a loaf of this wonderful bread by dinner.

DOUGH

- 1 cup plus 1 tablespoon and 1 teaspoon (200 g) Levain Starter (page 31)
- 3 cups plus 3 tablespoons (435 g) bread flour, plus more for dusting
- ¼ cup (30 g) whole wheat flour
- 2 tablespoons plus 1 teaspoon (15 g) rye flour
- 1 ¼ cups (300 ml) water, 78–82°F (26–28°C)
- 2 teaspoons (11 g) salt
- Olive oil, for greasing

MIX THE DOUGH. To mix by hand, place the starter, flours, water, and salt in a bowl and mix with your hands or a dough scraper until you have a smooth and soft dough. Pick up the dough with both hands and turn the dough out onto a floured surface. Squeeze the dough through your fingers until the dough is so firm that you can't squeeze it through your fingers anymore, about 5 minutes. Continue to work the dough by stretching the dough horizontally with your fingers and hands. Then fold each side into the center, one over another, to form a long rectangle about 5 by 15 inches (13 by 38 cm), like a three-panel brochure. Repeat, dusting with a little flour as necessary, until the dough is smooth and elastic, approximately 5 times.

To mix using a stand mixer, place the starter, flours, water, and salt in the bowl of a stand mixer fitted with a dough hook. Mix for

5 minutes on low speed (the 2 to 3 settings on a KitchenAid), scrape down the bowl and the dough hook, and then continue mixing for 5 minutes longer on medium speed (the 4 to 6 settings on a KitchenAid), or until the dough is smooth and elastic.

FIRST FERMENTATION. Transfer the dough to a stainless-steel bowl lightly greased with olive oil. Cover with a kitchen towel or plastic wrap and let rest for 3 hours at room temperature, above 72°F (22°C).

PRE-SHAPE AND REST TIME. Transfer the dough to a floured surface. Divide in half with a dough scraper. Using your hands, gently pat and guide each half into a round about 6 inches (15 cm) in diameter. Cover with a kitchen towel and let rest for another 15 minutes before the final forming.

FINAL FORMING. Dust your hands with flour. Use a dough scraper to lift the dough rounds off the floured surface to make sure they're not sticky. (If they are, gently brush your floured hands over the sticky places.) With your hands, pick up an edge of the dough and pull it to the center of the dough round. Make a quarter turn, fold the next edge to the center, and repeat this flattening, quarter turn, and repeat again. With your hands, gently smooth around the circumference. Repeat with the second dough round. Turn each round or boule over

so its smooth side is facing up. Each boule should be about 6 inches (15 cm) in diameter.

FINAL FERMENTATION. Dust the inside of 2 proofing baskets with flour. Place each formed boule, bottom side up, in the prepared proofing basket. Cover each boule loosely with plastic wrap and let proof for 3 hours at room temperature, above 72° F (22°C).

To prepare the oven for rebar steam baking, place an oven rack on the lowest rung of the oven. Arrange 10 small rebar in a single row along the bottom of a broiler pan; place the broiler pan on the lower oven rack. Arrange the second oven rack just above the broiler pan. Place a baking stone on the second, higher oven rack. After you put the loaf in the oven, pour ½ cup (120 ml) room-temperature water into the prepared broiler pan. Be careful of the hot steam. Quickly close the oven door.

To prepare the oven for cloche baking, place 1 oven rack on the lower third of the oven. Place a baking stone on the oven rack. Remove the second oven rack. When placing the boule in the oven, quickly invert a stainless-steel bowl over the loaf, creating a loose seal with the baking stone, and close the oven door. Remove the bowl after 10 minutes of baking to release the steam.

BAKE. After preparing the oven for either method of steam, preheat the oven to 450°F (232°C) for 3 hours. Lightly coat a wooden peel with flour. Gently place 1 boule on the prepared peel. With a bread lame or razor blade slanted at a 45-degree angle, make 3 horizontal and 3 vertical slashes (like a tic-tac-toe game), ⅛ to ¼ inch (3 to 6 mm) deep, across the top of each boule. Slide the boule off the oven peel onto the baking stone in the oven. (If using the rebar method, pour water into the broiler pan. If using the cloche method, place a stainless-steel bowl over the boule immediately after sliding the boule into the oven and remove the bowl after 10 minutes, as described above.) Total loaf bake time is 30 to 35 minutes, until the boule has turned a golden brown and sounds hollow when tapped on the bottom of the loaf in the center.

COOL ON A COOLING RACK. Repeat the baking process with the second loaf after allowing the oven and baking stone to come back to temperature, about 15 minutes. If the loaf is going to be eaten within 3 days, it is best kept on your countertop, unwrapped. The natural protection of the crusty exterior will preserve the soft interior crumb. For longer storage, wrap the loaf and store in the freezer. When ready to enjoy, thaw at room temperature and reheat in a 400°F (205°C) oven for 3 to 5 minutes.

KALAMATA OLIVE BOULE

Makes 2 round loaves or boules

Kalamata olive bread will make you feel like you are in Greece, sitting at the seaside and enjoying the sea breeze while relishing the taste of homemade olive-studded bread. Of course, this would be delicious with grilled fish or chicken, and it also makes a wonderful sandwich or addition to a cheese board. Remember: You can start this bread in the morning and enjoy by evening. You will also need 2 proofing baskets.

DOUGH

1 cup plus 1 tablespoon and 1 teaspoon (200 g) Levain Starter (page 31)

3 cups plus 3 tablespoons (435 g) bread flour, plus more for dusting

¼ cup (30 g) whole wheat flour

2 tablespoons plus 1 teaspoon (15 g) rye flour

1 ¼ cups (300 ml) water, 78–82°F (26–28°C)

2 teaspoons (11 g) salt

½ cup (100 g) chopped kalamata olives, patted dry

Olive oil, for greasing

MIX THE DOUGH. To mix by hand, place the starter, flours, water, and salt in a bowl and mix with your hands or a dough scraper until you have a smooth and soft dough. Pick up the dough with both hands and turn the dough out onto a floured surface. Squeeze the dough through your fingers until the dough is so firm that you can't squeeze it through your fingers anymore, about 5 minutes. Continue to work the dough by stretching the dough horizontally with your fingers and hands. Then fold each side into the center, one over another, to form a long rectangle about 5 by 15 inches (13 by 38 cm), like a three-panel brochure. Repeat, dusting with a little flour as necessary, until the dough is smooth and elastic, approximately 5 times.

To mix using a stand mixer, place the starter, flours, water, and salt in the bowl of a stand mixer fitted with a dough hook. Mix for 5 minutes on low speed (the 2 to 3 settings on a KitchenAid), scrape down the bowl and the dough hook, and then continue mixing for 5 minutes longer on medium speed (the 4 to 6 settings on a KitchenAid), or until the dough is smooth and elastic.

After the dough has been mixed, place it on a floured surface and pat down by hand, spreading the dough out. Sprinkle the olives over the surface and turn the dough over and over on itself with a dough scraper to form an olive-studded dough.

FIRST FERMENTATION. Transfer the dough to a stainless-steel bowl lightly greased with olive oil. Cover with a kitchen towel or plastic wrap and let rest for 3 hours at room temperature, above 72°F (22°C).

PRE-SHAPE AND REST TIME. Transfer the dough to a floured surface. Divide in half with a dough scraper. Using your hands, gently pat and guide each half into a round about 6 inches (15 cm) in diameter. Cover with a kitchen towel and let rest for another 15 minutes before the final forming.

FINAL FORMING. Dust your hands with flour. Use a dough scraper to lift the dough rounds off the floured surface to make sure they're not sticky. (If they are, gently brush your floured hands over the sticky places.) With your hands, pick up an edge of the dough and pull it to the center of the dough round. Make a quarter turn, fold the next edge to the center, and repeat this flattening, quarter turn, and repeat again. With your hands, gently smooth around the circumference. Repeat with the second dough round.

Turn each round or boule over so its smooth side is facing up. Each boule should be about 6 inches (15 cm) in diameter.

FINAL FERMENTATION. Dust the inside of 2 proofing baskets with flour. Place each formed boule, bottom side up, in the prepared proofing basket. Cover each boule loosely with plastic wrap and let proof for 3 hours at room temperature, above 72° F (22°C).

To prepare the oven for rebar steam baking, place an oven rack on the lowest rung of the oven. Arrange 10 small rebar in a single row along the bottom of a broiler pan; place the broiler pan on the lower oven rack. Arrange the second oven rack just above the broiler pan. Place a baking stone on the second, higher oven rack. After you put the loaf in the oven, pour ½ cup (120 ml) room-temperature water into the prepared broiler pan. Be careful of the hot steam. Quickly close the oven door.

To prepare the oven for cloche baking, place 1 oven rack on the lower third of the oven. Place a baking stone on the oven rack. Remove the second oven rack. When placing the boule in the oven, quickly invert a stainless-steel bowl over the loaf, creating a loose seal with the baking stone, and close the oven door. Remove the bowl after 10 minutes of baking to release the steam.

BAKE. After preparing the oven for either method of steam, preheat the oven to 450°F

(232°C) for 3 hours. Lightly coat a wooden peel with flour. Gently place 1 boule on the prepared peel. With a bread lame or razor blade slanted at a 45-degree angle, make 3 horizontal and 3 vertical slashes (like a tic-tac-toe game), ⅛ to ¼ inch (3 to 6 mm) deep, across the top of each boule. Slide the boule off the oven peel onto the baking stone in the oven. (If using the rebar method, pour water into the broiler pan. If using the cloche method, place a stainless-steel bowl over the boule immediately after sliding the boule into the oven and remove the bowl after 10 minutes, as described above.) Total loaf bake time is 30 to 35 minutes, until the boule has turned a golden brown and sounds hollow when tapped on the bottom of the loaf in the center.

COOL ON A COOLING RACK. Repeat the baking process with the second loaf after allowing the oven and baking stone to come back to temperature, about 15 minutes. If the loaf is going to be eaten within 3 days, it is best kept on your countertop, unwrapped. The natural protection of the crusty exterior will preserve the soft interior crumb. For longer storage, wrap the loaf and store in the freezer. When ready to enjoy, thaw at room temperature and reheat in a 400°F (205°C) oven for 3 to 5 minutes.

ROASTED-GARLIC BREAD

Makes 2 round loaves or boules

One whiff of this bread and the garlic lover enters heaven. There's no need to make separate garlic bread the next time you serve spaghetti—just serve up slices of this delicious loaf. Roast the garlic ahead of time, before you start making the dough. Just make sure the roasted garlic is at room temperature or warm before you mix it in the dough. You will need 2 proofing baskets to make this bread.

ROASTED GARLIC

½ cup (68 g) garlic cloves, peeled

1 tablespoon (15 ml) olive oil

DOUGH

1 cup plus 1 tablespoon and 1 teaspoon (200 g) Levain Starter (page 31)

3 cups plus 3 tablespoons (435 g) bread flour, plus more for dusting

¼ cup (30 g) whole wheat flour

2 tablespoons plus 1 teaspoon (15 g) rye flour

1 ¼ cups (300 ml) water, 78–82°F (26–28°C)

2 teaspoons (11 g) salt

Olive oil, for greasing

ROAST THE GARLIC. Preheat the oven to 350°F (177°C). Toss the garlic cloves in a small bowl with the olive oil to coat. Place on a baking sheet and roast for 10 minutes, or until just softened. Allow to cool.

MIX THE DOUGH. To mix by hand, place the starter, flours, water, and salt in a bowl and mix with your hands or a dough scraper until you have a smooth and soft dough. Pick up the dough with both hands and turn the dough out onto a floured surface. Squeeze the dough through your fingers until the dough is so firm that you can't squeeze it through your fingers anymore, about 5 minutes. Continue to work the dough by stretching the dough horizontally with your fingers and hands. Then fold each side into the center, one over another, to form a long rectangle about 5 by 15 inches (13 by 38 cm), like a three-panel brochure. Repeat, dusting with a little flour as necessary, until the dough is smooth and elastic, approximately 5 times.

To mix using a stand mixer, place the starter, flours, water, and salt in the bowl of a stand mixer fitted with a dough hook. Mix for

5 minutes on low speed (the 2 to 3 settings on a KitchenAid), scrape down the bowl and the dough hook, and then continue mixing for 5 minutes longer on medium speed (the 4 to 6 settings on a KitchenAid), or until the dough is smooth and elastic.

After the dough has been mixed, place it on a floured surface and pat down by hand, spreading the dough out. Sprinkle the garlic over the surface and turn the dough over and over on itself with a dough scraper to form a garlic-studded dough.

FIRST FERMENTATION. Transfer the dough to a stainless-steel bowl lightly greased with olive oil. Cover with a kitchen towel or plastic wrap and let rest for 3 hours at room temperature, above 72°F (22°C).

PRE-SHAPE AND REST TIME. Transfer the dough to a floured surface. Divide in half with a dough scraper. Using your hands, gently pat and guide each half into a round about 6 inches (15 cm) in diameter. Cover with a kitchen towel and let rest for another 15 minutes before the final forming.

FINAL FORMING. Dust your hands with flour. Use a dough scraper to lift the dough rounds off the floured surface to make sure they're not sticky. (If they are, gently brush your floured hands over the sticky places.) With your hands, pick up an edge of the dough and pull it to the center of the dough round. Make a quarter turn, fold the next edge to the center, and repeat this flattening, quarter turn, and repeat again. Cupping your hands, gently round the dough with pressure against the work surface. Repeat with the second dough rounds. Turn each round or boule over so its smooth side is facing up. Each boule should be about 6 inches (15 cm) in diameter.

PROOFING OR FINAL FERMENTATION. Dust the inside of 2 proofing baskets with flour. Place each formed boule, bottom side up, in the prepared proofing basket. Cover each boule loosely with plastic wrap and let proof for 3 hours at room temperature, above 72°F (22°C).

To prepare the oven for rebar steam baking, place an oven rack on the lowest rung of the oven. Arrange 10 small rebar in a single row along the bottom of a broiler pan; place the broiler pan on the lower oven rack. Arrange the second oven rack just above the broiler pan. Place a baking stone on the second, higher oven rack. After you put the loaf in the oven, pour ½ cup (120 ml) room-temperature water into the prepared broiler pan. Be careful of the hot steam. Quickly close the oven door.

To prepare the oven for cloche baking, place 1 oven rack on the lower third of the oven. Place a baking stone on the oven rack. Remove the second oven rack. When placing the boule in the oven, quickly invert a stainless-steel bowl over the loaf, creating a loose seal with the baking stone, and close the oven door. Remove the bowl after 10 minutes of baking to release the steam.

BAKE. After preparing the oven for either method of steam, preheat the oven to 450°F (232°C) for 3 hours. Lightly coat a wooden peel with flour. Gently place 1 boule on the prepared peel. With a bread lame or razor blade slanted at a 45-degree angle, make 3 horizontal and 3 vertical slashes (like a tic-tac-toe game), ⅛ to ¼ inch (3 to 6 mm) deep, across the top of each boule. Slide the boule off the oven peel onto the baking stone in the oven. (If using the rebar method, pour water into the broiler pan. If using the cloche method, place a stainless-steel bowl over the boule immediately after sliding the boule into the oven and remove the bowl after 10 minutes, as described above.) Total loaf bake time is 30 to 35 minutes, until the boule has turned a golden brown and sounds hollow when tapped on the bottom of the loaf in the center.

COOL ON A COOLING RACK. Repeat the baking process with the second loaf after allowing the oven and baking stone to come back to temperature, about 15 minutes. If the loaf is going to be eaten within 3 days, it is best kept on your countertop, unwrapped. The natural protection of the crusty exterior will preserve the soft interior crumb. For longer storage, wrap the loaf and store in the freezer. When ready to enjoy, thaw at room temperature and reheat in a 400°F (205°C) oven for 3 to 5 minutes.

SUN-DRIED TOMATO BOULE

Makes 2 round loaves or boules

All the wonder of summer is in this loaf. One bite and you are transported back to the relaxation of those sunny days no matter the time of year. This makes a great grilled cheese or bacon, lettuce, and double-tomato sandwich. You will need 2 proofing baskets and only a day of your time to make this bread.

DOUGH

1 cup plus 1 tablespoon and 1 teaspoon (200 g) Levain Starter (page 31)

3 cups plus 3 tablespoons (435 g) bread flour, plus more for dusting

¼ cup (30 g) whole wheat flour

2 tablespoons plus 1 teaspoon (15 g) rye flour

1 ¼ cups (300 ml) water, 78–82°F (26–28°C)

2 teaspoons (11 g) salt

1 cup (55 g) sun-dried tomatoes packed in oil, drained and cut into ½-inch (1 cm) pieces

2 teaspoons (5.5 g) roasted garlic

1 teaspoon (1 g) fresh oregano leaves, snipped

1 teaspoon (5 ml) olive oil, plus more for greasing

MIX THE DOUGH. To mix by hand, place the starter, flours, water, and salt in a bowl and mix with your hands or a dough scraper until you have a smooth and soft dough. Pick up the dough with both hands and turn the dough out onto a floured surface. Squeeze the dough through your fingers until the dough is so firm that you can't squeeze it through your fingers anymore, about 5 minutes. Continue to work the dough by stretching the dough horizontally with your fingers and hands. Then fold each side into the center, one over another, to form a long rectangle about 5 by 15 inches (13 by 38 cm), like a three-panel brochure. Repeat, dusting with a little flour as necessary, until the dough is smooth and elastic, approximately 5 times.

To mix using a stand mixer, place the starter, flours, water, and salt in the bowl of a stand mixer fitted with a dough hook. Mix for 5 minutes on low speed (the 2 to 3 settings on a KitchenAid), scrape down the bowl and the dough hook, and then continue mixing for 5 minutes longer on medium speed (the 4 to 6 settings on a KitchenAid), or until the dough is smooth and elastic.

(Continued on page 91)

After the dough has been mixed, place it on a floured surface and pat down by hand, spreading the dough out. Sprinkle the sun-dried tomatoes, garlic, oregano, and olive oil over the surface and turn the dough over and over on itself with a dough scraper to form a studded dough.

FIRST FERMENTATION. Transfer the dough to a stainless-steel bowl lightly greased with olive oil. Cover with a kitchen towel or plastic wrap and let rest for 3 hours at room temperature, above 72°F (22°C).

PRE-SHAPE AND REST TIME. Transfer the dough to a floured surface. Divide in half with a dough scraper. Using your hands, gently pat and guide each half into a round about 6 inches (15 cm) in diameter. Cover with a kitchen towel and let rest for another 15 minutes before the final forming.

FINAL FORMING. Dust your hands with flour. Use a dough scraper to lift the dough rounds off the floured surface to make sure they're not sticky. (If they are, gently brush your floured hands over the sticky places.) With your hands, pick up an edge of the dough and pull it to the center of the dough round. Make a quarter turn, fold the next edge to the center, and repeat this flattening, quarter turn, and repeat again. Cupping your hands, gently round the dough with pressure against the work surface. Repeat with the second dough round. Turn each round or boule over so its smooth side is facing up. Each boule should be about 6 inches (15 cm) in diameter.

FINAL FERMENTATION. Dust the inside of 2 proofing baskets with flour. Place each formed boule, bottom side up, in the prepared proofing basket. Cover each boule loosely with plastic wrap and let proof for 3 hours at room temperature, above 72°F (22°C).

To prepare the oven for rebar steam baking, place an oven rack on the lowest rung of the oven. Arrange 10 small rebar in a single row along the bottom of a broiler pan; place the broiler pan on the lower oven rack. Arrange the second oven rack just above the broiler pan. Place a baking stone on the second, higher oven rack. After you put the loaf in the oven, pour ½ cup (120 ml) room-temperature water into the prepared broiler pan. Be careful of the hot steam. Quickly close the oven door.

To prepare the oven for cloche baking, place 1 oven rack on the lower third of the oven. Place a baking stone on the oven rack. Remove the second oven rack. When placing the boule in the oven, quickly invert a stainless-steel bowl over the loaf, creating a loose seal with the baking stone, and close the oven door. Remove the bowl after 10 minutes of baking to release the steam.

BAKE. After preparing the oven for either method of steam, preheat the oven to 450°F (232°C) for 3 hours. Lightly coat a wooden peel with flour. Gently place 1 boule on the prepared peel. With a bread lame or razor blade slanted at a 45-degree angle, make 3 horizontal and 3 vertical slashes (like a tic-tac-toe game), ⅛ to ¼ inch (3 to 6 mm) deep, across the top of each boule. Slide the boule off the oven peel onto the baking stone in the oven. (If using the rebar method, pour water into the broiler pan. If using the cloche method, place a stainless-steel bowl over the boule immediately after sliding the boule into the oven and remove the bowl after 10 minutes, as described above.) Total loaf bake time is 30 to 35 minutes, until the boule has turned a golden brown and sounds hollow when tapped on the bottom of the loaf in the center.

COOL ON A COOLING RACK. Repeat the baking process with the second loaf after allowing the oven and baking stone to come back to temperature, about 15 minutes. If the loaf is going to be eaten within 3 days, it is best kept on your countertop, unwrapped. The natural protection of the crusty exterior will preserve the soft interior crumb. For longer storage, wrap the loaf and store in the freezer. When ready to enjoy, thaw at room temperature and reheat in a 400°F (205°C) oven for 3 to 5 minutes.

RAISIN-WALNUT BOULE

Makes 2 round loaves or boules

Breakfast just got better with a slice of homemade raisin-walnut bread. This nutty sweet bread is a treat in the morning, slathered with good butter, or served with an artisan Brie or a good local cheese. Because of the weight of the mix-in ingredients, this one takes longer to proof—12 to 16 hours. So, make this a 2-day project, but it is well worth the wait. Again, you will need 2 proofing baskets.

DOUGH

1 cup plus 1 tablespoon and 1 teaspoon (200 g) Levain Starter (page 31)

3 cups plus 3 tablespoons (435 g) bread flour, plus more for dusting

¼ cup (30 g) whole wheat flour

2 tablespoons plus 1 teaspoon (15 g) rye flour

1 ¼ cups (300 ml) water, 78–82°F (26–28°C)

2 teaspoons (11 g) salt

1 cup (150 g) raisins

½ cup plus 2 tablespoons (65 g) chopped walnuts

Olive oil, for greasing

MIX THE DOUGH. To mix by hand, place the starter, flours, water, and salt in a bowl and mix with your hands or a dough scraper until you have a smooth and soft dough. Pick up the dough with both hands and turn the dough out onto a floured surface. Squeeze the dough through your fingers until the dough is so firm that you can't squeeze it through your fingers anymore, about 5 minutes. Continue to work the dough by stretching the dough horizontally with your fingers and hands. Then fold each side into the center, one over another, to form a long rectangle about 5 by 15 inches (13 by 38 cm), like a three-panel brochure. Repeat, dusting with a little flour as necessary, until the dough is smooth and elastic, approximately 5 times.

To mix using a stand mixer, place the starter, flours, water, and salt in the bowl of a stand mixer fitted with a dough hook. Mix for 5 minutes on low speed (the 2 to 3 settings on a KitchenAid), scrape down the bowl and the dough hook, and then continue mixing for 5 minutes longer on medium speed (the 4 to 6 settings on a KitchenAid), or until the dough is smooth and elastic.

After the dough has been mixed, place it on a floured surface and pat down by hand, spreading the dough out. Sprinkle the raisins and walnuts over the surface and turn the dough over and over on itself with a dough scraper to form a studded dough.

FIRST FERMENTATION. Transfer the dough to a stainless-steel bowl lightly greased with olive oil. Cover with a kitchen towel or plastic wrap and let rest for 3 hours at room temperature, above 72°F (22°C).

PRE-SHAPE AND REST TIME. Transfer the dough to a floured surface. Divide in half with a dough scraper. Using your hands, gently pat and guide each half into a round about 6 inches (15 cm) in diameter. Cover with a kitchen towel and let rest for another 15 minutes before the final forming.

FINAL FORMING. Dust your hands with flour. Use a dough scraper to lift the dough rounds off the floured surface to make sure they're not sticky. (If they are, gently brush your floured hands over the sticky places.) With your hands, pick up an edge of the dough and pull it to the center of the dough round. Make a quarter turn, fold the next edge to the center, and repeat this flattening, quarter turn, and repeat again. Cupping your hands, gently round the dough with

pressure against the work surface. Repeat with the second dough round. Turn each round or boule over so its smooth side is facing up. Each boule should be about 6 inches (15 cm) in diameter.

FINAL FERMENTATION. Dust the inside of 2 proofing baskets with flour. Place each formed boule, bottom side up, in the prepared proofing basket. Cover each boule loosely with plastic wrap and let proof for 3 hours at 72°F (22°C).

To prepare the oven for rebar steam baking, place an oven rack on the lowest rung of the oven. Arrange 10 small rebar in a single row along the bottom of a broiler pan; place the broiler pan on the lower oven rack. Arrange the second oven rack just above the broiler pan. Place a baking stone on the second, higher oven rack. After you put the loaf in the oven, pour ½ cup (120 ml) room-temperature water into the prepared broiler pan. Be careful of the hot steam. Quickly close the oven door.

To prepare the oven for cloche baking, place 1 oven rack on the lower third of the oven. Place a baking stone on the oven rack. Remove the second oven rack. When placing the boule in the oven, quickly invert a stainless-steel bowl over the loaf, creating a loose seal with the baking stone, and close the oven door. Remove the bowl after 10 minutes of baking to release the steam.

BAKE. After preparing the oven for either method of steam, preheat the oven to 450°F (232°C) for 3 hours. Lightly coat a wooden peel with flour. Gently place 1 boule on the prepared peel. With a bread lame or razor blade slanted at a 45-degree angle, make 3 horizontal and 3 vertical slashes (like a tic-tac-toe game), ⅛ to ¼ inch (3 to 6 mm) deep, across the top of each boule. Slide the boule off the oven peel onto the baking stone in the oven. (If using the rebar method, pour water into the broiler pan. If using the cloche method, place a stainless-steel bowl over the boule immediately after sliding the boule into the oven and remove the bowl after 10 minutes, as described above.) Total loaf bake time is 30 to 35 minutes, until the boule has turned a golden brown and sounds hollow when tapped on the bottom of the loaf in the center.

COOL ON A COOLING RACK. Repeat the baking process with the second loaf after allowing the oven and baking stone to come back to temperature, about 15 minutes. If the loaf is going to be eaten within 3 days, it is best kept on your countertop, unwrapped. The natural protection of the crusty exterior will preserve the soft interior crumb. For longer storage, wrap the loaf and store in the freezer. When ready to enjoy, thaw at room temperature and reheat in a 400°F (205°C) oven for 3 to 5 minutes.

CHAPTER SIX

RYE

ONE OUT-OF-THE-ORDINARY BREAD we make in the bakery is our rye sourdough. Making this bread is a long process, like other sourdough breads.

Most Americans mistakenly associate caraway with rye flavor, but, rather, it adds a complementary flavor. When we add seeds to our rye bread—dill, fennel, chernushka (also known as nigella, tiny black seeds that taste a little like onion), sunflower, or flax—they are for additional flavor and color.

However, Farm to Market Bread Company bakes beautiful and tasty rye bread using 70 percent wheat flour and 30 percent rye flour and a rye starter that both leavens and flavors the bread. We also add a little vital wheat gluten, a powdery protein made from the gluten in wheat. Rye, lower in gluten, needs this extra help to create the strong and muscular structure that helps it rise.

We'll start with Deli Rye (page 98), then branch out with loaves such as Four-Seed Rye (page 101), Walnut–Green Onion Rye (page 105), and a fabulous Black Russian Rye (page 108) made with dark coffee concentrate.

DELI RYE BOULE

Makes 2 round loaves or boules

Our deli rye is a must-have for—you guessed it—deli-style sandwiches. The classic Reuben, ham and cheese, smoked turkey and provolone, or egg salad love this sturdy, wholesome, and slightly sour bread with a tender crumb. We use just a little bit of caraway seed for a flavor enhancer, not for the main flavor itself. Vital wheat gluten is a powdered protein made from wheat gluten, available with the specialty flours in the baking aisle of the grocery store or online.

DOUGH

1 cup plus 1 tablespoon and 1 teaspoon (200 g) Rye Starter (page 37)

2 ¼ cups plus 1 tablespoon (315 g) bread flour (page 21), plus more for dusting

1 cup (105 g) rye flour

1 ½ teaspoons (7 g) vital wheat gluten

1 ¼ cups (300 ml) water, 78–82°F (26–28°C)

1 tablespoon plus 1 teaspoon (13 g) caraway seeds

2 teaspoons (11 g) salt

Olive oil, for greasing

Cornmeal, for dusting

MIX THE DOUGH. To mix by hand, combine the starter, flours, vital wheat gluten, water, caraway seeds, and salt in a bowl and mix with your hands or a dough scraper until you have a smooth and soft dough. Pick up the dough with both hands and turn the dough out onto a floured surface. Squeeze the dough through your fingers until the dough is so firm that you can't squeeze it through your fingers anymore, about 5 minutes. Continue to work the dough by stretching the dough horizontally with your fingers and hands. Then fold each side into the center, one over another, to form a long rectangle about 5 by 15 inches (13 by 38 cm), like a three-panel brochure. Repeat, dusting with a little flour as necessary, until the dough is smooth and elastic, approximately 5 times.

To mix using a stand mixer, combine the starter, flours, vital wheat gluten, water, seeds, and salt in the bowl of a stand mixer fitted with a dough hook. Mix for 5 minutes on low speed (the 2 to 3 settings on a KitchenAid), scrape down the bowl and the dough hook, and continue mixing for 5 minutes longer on medium speed (the 4 to 6 settings on a KitchenAid), or until the dough is smooth and elastic.

FIRST FERMENTATION. Transfer the dough to a stainless-steel bowl lightly greased with olive oil. Cover with a kitchen towel and let rest for 3 hours at room temperature, above 72°F (22°C).

PRE-SHAPE AND REST TIME.
Transfer the dough to a floured surface. Divide in half with a dough scraper. Using your hands, gently pat and guide each half into a round about 6 inches (15 cm) in diameter. Cover with a kitchen towel and let rest for another 15 minutes before the final forming.

FINAL FORMING. Dust your hands with flour. Use a dough scraper to lift the dough rounds off the floured surface to make sure they're not sticky. If they are, gently brush your floured hands over the sticky places. With your hands, pick up an edge of the dough and pull it to the center of the dough round. Make a quarter turn, fold the next edge to the center, and repeat this flattening, quarter turn, and repeat again. Cupping your hands, gently round the dough with pressure against the work surface. Repeat with the second dough round. Turn each round or boule over so its smooth side is facing up. Each boule should be about 6 inches (15 cm) in diameter.

FINAL FERMENTATION. Dust the inside of 2 proofing baskets with flour. Place each formed boule, bottom side up, in the prepared proofing basket. Cover each boule with loose plastic wrap and let proof for 3 hours at room temperature, above 72°F (22°C).

To prepare the oven for rebar steam baking, place an oven rack on the lowest rung of the oven. Arrange 10 small rebar in a single row along the bottom of a broiler pan; place the broiler pan on the lower oven rack. Arrange the second oven rack just above the broiler pan. Place a baking stone on the second, higher oven rack. After you put the loaf in the oven, pour ½ cup (120 ml) room-temperature water into the prepared broiler pan. Be careful of the hot steam. Quickly close the oven door.

To prepare the oven for cloche baking, place 1 oven rack on the lower third of the oven. Place a baking stone on the oven rack. Remove the second oven rack. When placing the boule in the oven, quickly invert a stainless-steel bowl over the loaf, creating a loose seal with the baking stone, and close the oven door. Remove the bowl after 10 minutes of baking to release the steam.

BAKE. After preparing the oven for either method of steam, preheat the oven to 450°F (232°C) for 3 hours. Lightly coat a wooden peel with cornmeal. Gently place 1 boule on the prepared peel. With a bread lame or razor blade slanted at a 45-degree angle, make 3 horizontal and 3 vertical slashes (like a tic-tac-toe game), ⅛ to ¼ inch (3 to 6 mm) deep, across the top of each boule. Slide the boule off the oven peel onto the baking stone in the oven. (If using the rebar method, pour water into the broiler pan. If using the cloche method, place a stainless-steel bowl over the boule immediately after sliding the boule into the oven and remove the bowl after 10 minutes, as described above.) Total loaf bake time is 30 to 35 minutes, until the boule has turned a golden brown and sounds hollow when tapped on the bottom of the loaf in the center.

COOL ON A COOLING RACK. Repeat the baking process with the second loaf after allowing the oven and baking stone to come back to temperature, around 15 minutes. If the loaf is going to be eaten within 3 days, it is best kept on your countertop, unwrapped. The natural protection of the crusty exterior will preserve the soft interior crumb. For longer storage, wrap the loaf and store in the freezer. When ready to enjoy, thaw at room temperature and reheat in a 400°F (205°C) oven for 3 to 5 minutes.

FOUR-SEED RYE

Makes 2 round loaves or boules

Four seeds—sunflower seed kernels, sesame seeds, poppy seeds, and flaxseeds—make this a delicious rye bread with just that little bit of extra texture. This is a great bread for an artisan butter, a smooth spread, or a schmear of cream cheese. You can find vital wheat gluten with the specialty flours in the baking aisle of grocery stores and the seeds in the bulk section.

DOUGH

1 cup plus 1 tablespoon and 1 teaspoon (200 g) Rye Starter (page 37)

2 ¼ cups plus 1 tablespoon (315 g) bread flour (page 21), plus more for dusting

1 cup (105 g) rye flour

1 ½ teaspoons (7 g) vital wheat gluten

1 ¼ cups (300 ml) water, 78–82°F (26–28°C)

2 teaspoons (11 g) salt

⅓ cup (50 g) roasted sunflower seed kernels

2 tablespoons (20 g) sesame seeds

1 tablespoon (10 g) poppy seeds

1 tablespoon (10 g) flaxseeds

Olive oil, for greasing

Cornmeal, for dusting

MIX THE DOUGH. To mix by hand, place the starter, flours, vital wheat gluten, water, salt, and seeds in a bowl and mix with your hands or a dough scraper until you have a smooth and soft dough. Pick up the dough with both hands and turn the dough out onto a floured surface. Squeeze the dough through your fingers until the dough is so firm that you can't squeeze it through your fingers anymore, about 5 minutes. Continue to work the dough by stretching the dough horizontally with your fingers and hands. Then fold each side into the center, one over another, to form a long rectangle about 5 by 15 inches (13 by 38 cm), like a three-panel brochure. Repeat, dusting with a little flour as necessary, until the dough is smooth and elastic, approximately 5 times.

To mix using a stand mixer, place the starter, flours, vital wheat gluten, water, salt, and seeds in the bowl of a stand mixer fitted with a dough hook. Mix for 5 minutes on low speed (the 2 to 3 settings on a KitchenAid), scrape down the bowl and the dough hook, and continue mixing for 5 minutes longer on medium speed (the 4 to 6 settings on

(Continued on page 103)

a KitchenAid), or until the dough is smooth and elastic.

FIRST FERMENTATION. Transfer the dough to a stainless-steel bowl lightly greased with olive oil. Cover with a kitchen towel and let rest for 3 hours at room temperature, above 72°F (22°C).

PRE-SHAPE AND REST TIME. Transfer the dough to a floured surface. Divide in half with a dough scraper. Using your hands, gently pat and guide each half into a round about 6 inches (15 cm) in diameter. Cover with a kitchen towel and let rest for another 15 minutes before the final forming.

FINAL FORMING. Dust your hands with flour. Use a dough scraper to lift the dough rounds off the floured surface to make sure they're not sticky. If they are, gently brush your floured hands over the sticky places. With your hands, pick up an edge of the dough and pull it to the center of the dough round. Make a quarter turn, fold the next edge to the center, and repeat this flattening, quarter turn, and repeat again. Cupping your hands, gently round the dough with pressure against the work surface. Repeat with the second dough round. Turn each round or boule over so its smooth side is facing up. Each boule should be about 6 inches (15 cm) in diameter.

FINAL FERMENTATION. Dust the inside of 2 proofing baskets with flour.

Place each formed boule, bottom side up, in the prepared proofing basket. Cover each boule loosely with plastic wrap and let proof for 3 hours at room temperature, above 72°F (22°C).

To prepare the oven for rebar steam baking, place an oven rack on the lowest rung of the oven. Arrange 10 small rebar in a single row along the bottom of a broiler pan; place the broiler pan on the lower oven rack. Arrange the second oven rack just above the broiler pan. Place a baking stone on the second, higher oven rack. After you put the loaf in the oven, pour ½ cup (120 ml) room-temperature water into the prepared broiler pan. Be careful of the hot steam. Quickly close the oven door.

To prepare the oven for cloche baking, place 1 oven rack on the lower third of the oven. Place a baking stone on the oven rack. Remove the second oven rack. When placing the boule in the oven, quickly invert a stainless-steel bowl over the loaf, creating a loose seal with the baking stone, and close the oven door. Remove the bowl after 10 minutes of baking to release the steam.

BAKE. After preparing the oven for either method of steam, preheat the oven to 450°F (232°C) for 3 hours. Lightly coat a wooden peel with cornmeal. Gently place 1 boule on the prepared peel. With a bread lame or razor blade slanted at a 45-degree angle, make 3 horizontal and 3 vertical slashes (like a tic-tac-toe game), ⅛ to ¼ inch

(3 to 6 mm) deep, across the top of each boule. Slide the boule off the oven peel onto the baking stone in the oven. (If using the rebar method, pour water into the broiler pan. If using the cloche method, place a stainless-steel bowl over the boule immediately after sliding the boule into the oven and remove the bowl after 10 minutes, as described above.) Total loaf bake time is 30 to 35 minutes, until the boule has turned a golden brown and sounds hollow when tapped on the bottom of the loaf in the center.

COOL ON A COOLING RACK. Repeat the baking process with the second loaf after allowing the oven and baking stone to come back to temperature, about 15 minutes. If the loaf is going to be eaten within 3 days, it is best kept on your countertop, unwrapped. The natural protection of a crusty exterior will preserve the soft interior crumb. For longer storage, wrap the loaf and store in the freezer. When ready to enjoy, thaw at room temperature and reheat in a 400°F (205°C) oven for 3 to 5 minutes.

WALNUT-GREEN ONION
RYE BATARD

Makes 2 round loaves or batards

The mild onion flavor and slight crunch of walnuts make this bread a worthy addition to our rye bread family. It's delicious toasted and then spread with good butter, but it also makes a fabulous grilled cheese with Havarti, aged cheddar, or Brie and bacon. You can form and bake this as a boule, as in the previous recipes, or do it as a batard, as here.

DOUGH

- 1 cup plus 1 tablespoon and 1 teaspoon (200 g) Rye Starter (page 37)
- 2 ¼ cups plus 1 tablespoon (315 g) bread flour (page 21), plus more for dusting
- 1 cup (105 g) rye flour
- 1 ½ teaspoons (7 g) vital wheat gluten
- 1 ¼ cups (300 ml) water, 78–82°F (26–28°C)
- 2 teaspoons (11 g) salt
- ¼ cup plus 2 teaspoons (45 g) chopped walnuts
- 2 tablespoons (20 g) chopped green onion (including green and white parts)
- Olive oil, for greasing
- Cornmeal, for dusting

MIX THE DOUGH. To mix by hand, place the starter, flours, vital wheat gluten, water, salt, walnuts, and green onion in a bowl and mix with your hands or a dough scraper until you have a smooth and soft dough. Pick up the dough with both hands and turn the dough out onto a floured surface. Squeeze the dough through your fingers until the dough is so firm that you can't squeeze it through your fingers anymore, about 5 minutes. Continue to work the dough by stretching the dough horizontally with your fingers and hands. Then fold each side into the center, one over another, to form a long rectangle about 5 by 15 inches (13 by 38 cm), like a three-panel brochure. Repeat, dusting with a little flour as necessary, until the dough is smooth and elastic, approximately 5 times.

To mix using a stand mixer, place the starter, flours, vital wheat gluten, water, salt, walnuts, and green onion in the bowl of a stand mixer fitted with a dough hook. Mix for 5 minutes on low speed (the 2 to 3 settings on a KitchenAid), scrape down the bowl and the dough hook, and continue mixing for 5 minutes on medium speed (the 4 to 6 settings on a KitchenAid), or until the dough is smooth and elastic.

FIRST FERMENTATION. Transfer the dough to a stainless-steel bowl lightly greased with olive oil. Cover with a kitchen towel or plastic wrap and let rest for 3 hours at room temperature, above 72°F (22°C).

PRE-SHAPE AND REST TIME. Transfer the dough to a floured surface. With the flat of your hand, press the dough into a round. Divide in half with a dough scraper. Using your hands, gently pat and guide each half into an oblong shape. Place the pieces on a floured work surface, seam side up. Cover with a floured kitchen towel and let rest for another 15 minutes before the final forming.

FINAL FORMING. Dust your hands with flour. Use a dough scraper to lift the dough pieces off the floured surface to begin final forming. Pat down in a long oval shape, with the long portion oriented vertically. Fold the top one-third of the dough toward you and pat down. Take the top 2 corners of the shape and bring them to the center of the dough. Pat out the air. Turn the dough 180 degrees, repeat by folding the top one-third of the dough toward you, and pat down. Take the top 2 corners of the shape and bring them into the center of the dough. Pat out the air. Hold the dough with your fingers on the back side of the dough and push the dough against the work surface with your thumbs, creating a seam. Touch up the shape of the dough by gently rolling the oval until the desired shape is achieved. Each oblong shape should be about 4 by 12 inches (10 by 30.5 cm).

FINAL FERMENTATION. Dust the work surface with flour and place each formed batard, bottom side up, on the surface. Cover loosely with a kitchen towel and let proof for 3 hours at room temperature, above 72°F (22°C).

To prepare the oven for rebar steam baking, place an oven rack on the lowest rung of the oven. Arrange 10 small rebar in a single row along the bottom of a broiler pan; place the broiler pan on the lower oven rack. Arrange the second oven rack just above the broiler pan. Place a baking stone on the second, higher oven rack. After you put the loaf in the oven, pour ½ cup (120 ml) room-temperature water into the prepared broiler pan. Be careful of the hot steam. Quickly close the oven door.

To prepare the oven for cloche baking, place 1 oven rack on the lower third of the oven. Place a baking stone on the oven rack. Remove the second oven rack. When placing the loaf in the oven, quickly invert a stainless-steel bowl over the loaf, creating a loose seal with the baking stone, and close the oven door. Remove the bowl after 10 minutes of baking to release the steam.

BAKE. After preparing the oven for either method of steam, preheat the oven to 450°F (232°C) for 3 hours. Lightly coat a wooden peel with cornmeal. Gently place 1 batard on the prepared peel. With a bread lame or razor blade slanted at a 45-degree angle, make 3 diagonal slashes ⅛ to ¼ inch (3 to 6 mm) deep across the top of each loaf. Slide theloaf off the oven peel onto the baking stone in the oven. (If using the rebar method, pour water into the broiler pan. If using the cloche method, place a stainless-steel bowl over the loaf immediately after sliding the loaf into the oven and remove the bowl after 10 minutes, as described above.) Total loaf bake time is 30 to 35 minutes, until the batard has turned a golden brown and sounds hollow when tapped on the bottom of the loaf in the center.

COOL ON A COOLING RACK. Repeat the baking process with the second loaf after allowing the oven and baking stone to come back to temperature, about 15 minutes. If the loaf is going to be eaten within 3 days, it is best kept on your countertop, unwrapped. The natural protection of the crusty exterior will preserve the soft interior crumb. For longer storage, wrap the loaf and store in the freezer. When ready to enjoy, thaw at room temperature and reheat in a 400°F (205°C) oven for 3 to 5 minutes.

BLACK RUSSIAN RYE

Makes 2 round loaves or boules

For rye bread lovers, this is the quintessential loaf. There are many ways to achieve a dark rye bread. Most American bakeries use a dark caramel color. German bakers attain the dark-colored pumpernickel by baking the bread in a steam chamber for 16 hours. This recipe uses strong brewed coffee and Dutch-process cocoa powder for a dark rye. Our favorite coffee is cold-brewed Toddy coffee concentrate, but any strong brewed dark-roast coffee that has come to room temperature is fine. You can also find bottled cold-brew coffee concentrate at places like Trader Joe's. For this bread, as in the San Francisco Sourdough Boule (page 58), you will start with a sponge.

SPONGE

¾ cup plus 2 tablespoons (165 g) Rye Starter (page 37)

¾ cup plus 1 tablespoon (110 g) bread flour (page 21)

½ cup plus 1 teaspoon (55 g) rye flour

⅓ cup plus 1 teaspoon (85 ml) strong brewed coffee, at room temperature, or Toddy coffee concentrate

2 tablespoons (20 g) granulated sugar

DOUGH

¾ cup plus 1 tablespoon (110 g) bread flour (page 21), plus more for dusting

⅓ cup plus 2 tablespoons and 1 teaspoon (50 g) rye flour

1 ½ teaspoons (7 g) vital wheat gluten

1 ½ teaspoons (5 g) Dutch-process cocoa powder

1 cup plus 2 tablespoons (270 ml) strong brewed coffee, at room temperature

2 teaspoons (8 ml) olive oil, plus more for greasing

3 tablespoons (35 g) granulated sugar

1 teaspoon (5.5 g) salt

½ cup (75 g) small raisins

1 ½ cups (350 g) Sponge

Cornmeal, for dusting

PREPARE THE SPONGE. In a large stainless-steel bowl, place the starter, flours, coffee, and sugar. Mix together with your hands until you have a smooth mass, about 2 minutes. It's important not to overmix the sponge. Cover with plastic wrap and allow to rise at room temperature until almost doubled in volume, 3 to 5 hours.

MIX THE DOUGH. To mix by hand, add the flours, vital wheat gluten, cocoa powder, coffee, olive oil, sugar, salt, and raisins to the sponge. Mix with your hands or a dough scraper until you have a smooth and soft dough. Pick up the dough with both hands and turn the dough out onto a floured surface. Squeeze the dough through your fingers until the dough is so firm that you can't squeeze it through your fingers anymore, about 5 minutes. Continue to work the dough by stretching the dough horizontally with your fingers and hands. Then fold each side into the center, one over another, to form a long rectangle about 5 by 15 inches (13 by 38 cm), like a three-panel brochure. Repeat, dusting with a little flour as necessary, until the dough is smooth and elastic, approximately 5 times.

To mix using a stand mixer, transfer the sponge to the bowl of a stand mixer fitted with a dough hook and add the flours, vital wheat gluten, cocoa powder, coffee, olive oil, sugar salt, and raisins. Mix for 5 minutes on low speed (the 2 to 3 settings on a KitchenAid), scrape down the bowl and the dough hook, and then continue mixing for 5 minutes longer on medium speed (the 4 to 6 settings on a KitchenAid), or until the dough is smooth and elastic.

FIRST FERMENTATION. Transfer the dough to a stainless-steel bowl lightly greased with olive oil. Cover with a kitchen towel and let rest for 3 hours at room temperature, above 72°F (22°C).

PRE-SHAPE AND REST TIME. Transfer the dough to a floured surface. Divide in half with a dough scraper. Using your hands, gently pat and guide each half into a round about 6 inches (15 cm) in diameter. Cover with a kitchen towel and let rest for another 15 minutes before the final forming.

FINAL FORMING. Dust your hands with flour. Use a dough scraper to lift the dough rounds off the floured surface to make sure they're not sticky. (If they are, gently brush your floured hands over the sticky places.) With your hands, pick up an edge of the dough and pull it to the center of the dough round. Make a quarter turn, fold the next edge to the center, and repeat this flattening, quarter turn, and repeat again. Cupping your hands, gently round the dough with pressure against the work surface. Repeat with the second dough round. Turn each round or boule over so its smooth side is facing up. Each boule should be about 6 inches (15 cm) in diameter.

FINAL FERMENTATION. Place the formed boules on a cornmeal-covered surface. Cover each boule with loose plastic wrap and let proof for 3 hours at room temperature, above 72°F (22°C).

To prepare the oven for rebar steam baking, place an oven rack on the lowest rung of the oven. Arrange 10 small rebar in a single row along the bottom of a broiler pan; place the broiler pan on the lower oven rack. Arrange the second oven rack just above the broiler pan. Place a baking stone on the second, higher oven rack. After you put the loaf in the oven, pour ½ cup (120 ml) room-temperature water into the prepared broiler pan. Be careful of the hot steam. Quickly close the oven door.

To prepare the oven for cloche baking, place 1 oven rack on the lower third of the oven. Place a baking stone on the oven rack. Remove the second oven rack. When placing the boule in the oven, quickly invert a stainless-steel bowl over the loaf, creating a loose seal with the baking stone, and close the oven door. Remove the bowl after 10 minutes of baking to release the steam.

BAKE. After preparing the oven for either method of steam, preheat the oven to 375°F (191°C) for 3 hours. Lightly coat a wooden peel with cornmeal. Gently place 1 boule on the prepared peel. With a bread lame or razor blade slanted at a 45-degree angle, make 3 horizontal and 3 vertical slashes

(like a tic-tac-toe game), ⅛ to ¼ inch (3 to 6 mm) deep, across the top of each boule. Slide the boule off the oven peel onto the baking stone in the oven. (If using the rebar method, pour water into the broiler pan. If using the cloche method, place a stainless-steel bowl over the boule immediately after sliding the boule into the oven and remove the bowl after 10 minutes, as described above.) Total loaf bake time is 30 to 35 minutes, until the boule has turned a golden brown and sounds hollow when tapped on the bottom of the loaf in the center.

COOL ON A COOLING RACK. Repeat the baking process with the second loaf after allowing the oven and baking stone to come back to temperature, about 15 minutes. If the loaf is going to be eaten within 3 days, it is best kept on your countertop, unwrapped. The natural protection of the crusty exterior will preserve the soft interior crumb. For longer storage, wrap the loaf and store in the freezer. When ready to enjoy, thaw at room temperature and reheat in a 400°F (205°C) oven for 3 to 5 minutes.

GOLDEN ONION
RYE BATARD

Makes 2 round loaves or batards

Sautéing onions until golden, then adding them to the rye bread dough creates a bread with savory sweetness. Bread this good needs to be savored down to the last crust. Leftovers would make great croutons for a French onion soup or a Caesar salad—just cut the bread into cubes, drizzle with a little olive oil, and bake in a 350°F (177°C) oven until crisp, about 20 minutes.

GOLDEN ONIONS

1 large yellow onion, finely chopped

2 tablespoons (30 ml) olive oil

DOUGH

1 cup plus 1 tablespoon and 1 teaspoon (200 g) Rye Starter (page 37)

2 ¼ cups plus 1 tablespoon (315 g) bread flour (page 21), plus more for dusting

1 cup (105 g) rye flour

1 ½ teaspoons (7 g) vital wheat gluten

1 ¼ cups (300 ml) water, 78–82°F (26–28°C)

2 teaspoons (11 g) salt

Olive oil, for greasing

Cornmeal, for dusting

PREPARE THE GOLDEN ONIONS. In a skillet on medium heat, sauté the onion in the olive oil until golden, about 10 minutes. Set aside to cool.

MIX THE DOUGH. To mix by hand, place the starter, flours, vital wheat gluten, water, salt, and sautéed onions in a bowl and mix with your hands or a dough scraper until you have a smooth and soft dough. Pick up the dough with both hands and turn the dough out onto a floured surface. Squeeze the dough through your fingers until the dough is so firm that you can't squeeze it through your fingers anymore, about 5 minutes. Continue to work the dough by stretching the dough horizontally with your fingers and hands. Then fold each side into the center, one over another, to form a long rectangle about 5 by 15 inches (13 by 38 cm), like a three-panel brochure. Repeat, dusting with a little flour as necessary, until the dough is smooth and elastic, approximately 5 times.

To mix using a stand mixer, place the starter, flours, vital wheat gluten, water, salt, and sautéed onions in the bowl of a stand mixer fitted with a dough hook. Mix for 5 minutes on low speed (the 2 to 3 settings on a KitchenAid), scrape down the bowl and the dough hook, and then continue mixing for 5 minutes longer on medium speed (the 4 to 6 settings on a KitchenAid), or until the dough is smooth and elastic.

FIRST FERMENTATION. Transfer the dough to a stainless-steel bowl lightly greased with olive oil. Cover with a kitchen towel and let rest for 3 hours at room temperature, above 72°F (22°C).

PRE-SHAPE AND REST TIME. Transfer the dough to a floured surface. With the flat of your hand, press the dough into a round. Divide in half with a dough scraper. Using your hands, gently pat and guide each half into an oblong shape. Place the pieces on a floured work surface, seam side up. Cover with a floured kitchen towel and let rest for another 15 minutes before the final forming.

FINAL FORMING. Dust your hands with flour. Use a dough scraper to lift the dough pieces off the floured surface to begin the final forming. Pat down in a long oval shape, with the long portion oriented vertically. Fold the top one-third of the dough toward you and pat down. Take the top 2 corners of the shape and bring them to the center of the dough. Pat out the air. Turn the dough 180 degrees, repeat by folding

the top one-third of the dough toward you, and pat down. Take the top 2 corners of the shape and bring them into the center of the dough. Pat out the air. Hold the dough with your fingers on the back side of the dough and push the dough against the work surface with your thumbs, creating a seam. Touch up the shape of the dough by gently rolling the oval until the desired shape is achieved. Each oblong shape should be about 4 by 12 inches (10 by 30.5 cm).

FINAL FERMENTATION. Dust the work surface with flour and place each formed batard, bottom side up, on the surface. Cover loosely with a kitchen towel and let proof for 3 hours at room temperature, above 72°F (22°C).

To prepare the oven for rebar steam baking, place an oven rack on the lowest rung of the oven. Arrange 10 small rebar in a single row along the bottom of a broiler pan; place the broiler pan on the lower oven rack. Arrange the second oven rack just above the broiler pan. Place a baking stone on the second, higher oven rack. After you put the loaf in the oven, pour ½ cup (120 ml) room-temperature water into the prepared broiler pan. Be careful of the hot steam. Quickly close the oven door.

To prepare the oven for cloche baking, place 1 oven rack on the lower third of the oven. Place a baking stone on the oven rack. Remove the second oven rack. When placing the loaf in the oven, quickly invert

a stainless-steel bowl over the loaf, creating a loose seal with the baking stone, and close the oven door. Remove the bowl after 10 minutes of baking to release the steam.

BAKE. After preparing the oven for either method of steam, preheat the oven to 450°F (232°C) for 3 hours. Lightly coat a wooden peel with cornmeal. Gently place 1 batard on the prepared peel. With a bread lame or razor blade slanted at a 45-degree angle, make 3 diagonal slashes ⅛ to ¼ inch (3 to 6 mm) deep, across the top of each loaf. Slide the loaf off the oven peel onto the baking stone in the oven. (If using the rebar method, pour water into the broiler pan. If using the cloche method, place a stainless-steel bowl over the loaf immediately after sliding the loaf into the oven and remove the bowl after 10 minutes, as described above.) Total loaf bake time is 30 to 35 minutes, until the batard has turned a golden brown and sounds hollow when tapped on the bottom of the loaf in the center.

COOL ON A COOLING RACK. Repeat the baking process with the second loaf after allowing the oven and baking stone to come back to temperature, about 15 minutes. If the loaf is going to be eaten within 3 days, it is best kept on your countertop, unwrapped. The natural protection of the crusty exterior will preserve the soft interior crumb. For longer storage, wrap the loaf and store in the freezer. When ready to enjoy, thaw at room temperature and reheat in a 400°F (205°C) oven for 3 to 5 minutes

CHAPTER SEVEN

BIGA, THE ITALIAN
PRE-FERMENT

IN THE EARLY 1900s, use of packaged yeast became more widespread, giving bakers an alternative to slow-baked breads from starters. With the convenience of that faster rise time came problems. The bread lacked texture and flavor. Bakers searched for a way that these problems could be eliminated while still using the yeast and faster rise time. A solution was found with biga, a pre-ferment that helped bakers deal with the absence of sourdough starter and resulting loss of flavor.

Today, we make biga with another baking improvement—instant dry yeast. This yeast with a finer granule is meant to mix right in with the dough; you don't have to add this yeast to water first. I like to use SAF instant yeast in biga. You can find SAF yeast at better grocery stores, kitchen shops, or online at places like www.kingarthur.com.

As you'll learn, biga can serve a unique place in your baking. Unlike longer fermenting starters, biga is made fresh. Biga is made using a small amount of baker's yeast in a thick dough that varies from 45 to 60 percent hydration and is fermented from 12 to 16 hours to fully develop its unique taste. After the first 2 hours of fermentation, place in the refrigerator and use the following day.

Many regional classic breads begin with biga. Italian baking makes use of this pre-ferment. Although not a naturally and slowly fermented starter, biga is made from flour, water, and yeast and allowed to ferment. This pre-ferment helps loaves remain fresher and taste sweeter than those made with a large amount of yeast.

Biga is hearty and produces a bread with complex flavors as well as a light, open texture with holes. Compared to the Levain Starter (page 31), it is thicker and easier to work with. The thickness of the biga is believed to give loaves made with it a characteristic slightly nutty taste.

Initially, biga will look rather unimpressive; however, give it a few hours and the dough will soften and hydrate. Biga is ripe when the dough has risen and is just beginning to recede in the center. One of the best things about biga is that it offers a lot of flavor and many of the qualities of sour starters without the time commitment.

HOW TO MAKE A BIGA

Makes 2 cups

Make a batch of biga, then weigh out the amount you will need for each recipe in this chapter. Cover and freeze the rest for up to 3 months for another day's baking.

INGREDIENTS

2 cups plus 3 tablespoons (300 g) bread flour

¾ cup (180 ml) water, 78–82°F (26–28°C)

¼ teaspoon (0.75 g) instant yeast

Stir all of the ingredients together in a large bowl until smooth. Ferment for 16 hours.

CIABATTA

Makes 2 loaves

Ciabatta (the name is Italian for *slipper*) is traditionally formed in the shape of a ballet slipper—long, wide, and somewhat flat. After it is mixed, we give the dough 3 hours to allow the fermentation process to make those bubbles, and we stretch and fold the dough once to strengthen the gluten. The result is a long loaf with a crisp crust and an open crumb.

It is great sliced for panini or cut in half horizontally for a loaf sandwich to feed a crowd. Slices of ciabatta are also great for making crostini or bruschetta. Ciabatta dough is sticky and floppy, so it requires a light touch. Be sure to work it and shape it the least amount possible. It will firm up during baking. You will need a couche or a strong linen towel, floured, for the ciabatta to rest for its final proofing. You will also need cornmeal to sprinkle on the wooden peel so that this loaf will slide off easier. With the biga made the night before, this is a bread you can make in 1 day, with two proofing times for the dough.

DOUGH

- 1 cup plus 1 tablespoon and 1 teaspoon (200 g) Biga (page 116)

- 3 cups plus 3 tablespoons and 1 teaspoon (440 g) bread flour, plus more for dusting

- 2 teaspoons (11 g) salt

- ⅓ teaspoon (1 g) instant yeast

- 1 ½ cups plus 1 tablespoon (375 ml) water, 78–82°F (26–28°C)

- Olive oil, for greasing

- Cornmeal, for dusting

MIX THE DOUGH. To mix by hand, place the biga, flour, salt, yeast, and water in a bowl and mix with your hands or a dough scraper until you have a smooth and soft dough. Using a plastic scraper, empty the dough out onto a floured surface. Squeeze the dough through your fingers until the dough is so firm that you can't squeeze it through your fingers anymore, about 5 minutes. Continue to work the dough by stretching the dough horizontally with your fingers and hands. Then fold each side into the center, one over another, to form a long rectangle about 5 by 15 inches (13 by 38 cm), like a three-panel brochure. Repeat, dusting with a little flour as necessary, until the dough is smooth and elastic, approximately 5 times.

To mix using a stand mixer, place the starter, flour, salt, yeast, and water in the bowl of a stand mixer fitted with a dough hook. Mix for 5 minutes on low speed (the 2 to 3 settings on a KitchenAid). Continue mixing for 5 minutes longer on medium speed (the 4 to 6 settings on a KitchenAid), or until the dough is smooth and elastic.

FIRST FERMENTATION. Transfer the dough to a stainless-steel bowl lightly greased with olive oil. Cover with a kitchen towel or plastic wrap and let rest for 3 hours at room temperature, above 72°F (22°C).

SHAPE AND FINAL FERMENTATION. Transfer the dough to a floured surface. With the flat of your hand, press the dough into a square. Divide in half with a dough scraper. Using your hands, gently pat and guide each half into a long rectangle about 4 by 12 inches (10 by 30 cm). Be especially careful with this loaf to not fully de-gas and lose air bubbles. Transfer the first rectangle to a floured couche. To keep the dough pieces separated, use your fingers to pinch up a long ridge of the couche along the inner edge of the dough. Transfer the second rectangle to the couche. Cover with a floured kitchen towel and let rest for another 1 ½ hours at room temperature before baking.

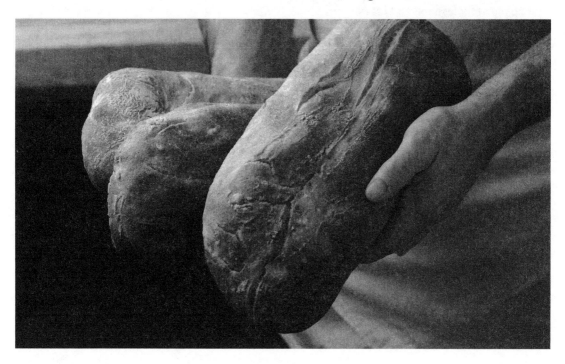

To prepare the oven for rebar steam baking, place an oven rack on the lowest rung of the oven. Arrange 10 small rebar in a single row along the bottom of a broiler pan; place the broiler pan on the lower oven rack. Arrange the second oven rack just above the broiler pan. Place a baking stone on the second, higher oven rack. After you load the loaf in the oven, pour ½ cup (120 ml) room-temperature water into the prepared broiler pan. Be careful of the hot steam. Quickly close the oven door.

To prepare the oven for cloche baking, place 1 oven rack on the lower third of the oven. Place a baking stone on the oven rack. Remove the second oven rack. When placing the loaf in the oven, quickly invert a stainless-steel bowl over the loaf, creating a loose seal with the baking stone, and close the oven door. Remove the bowl after 10 minutes of baking to release the steam.

BAKE. After preparing the oven for either method of steam, preheat the oven to 450°F (232°C) for 3 hours. Lightly coat a wooden peel with cornmeal. Gently place 1 rectangle on the prepared peel with the bottom side up. Slide the loaf off the oven peel onto the baking stone in the oven. (If using the rebar method, pour water into the broiler pan. If using the cloche method, place a stainless-steel bowl over the loaf immediately after sliding the loaf into the oven and remove the bowl after 10 minutes, as described above.) Total loaf bake time is 30 to 35 minutes, until the loaf has turned a golden brown and sounds hollow when tapped on the bottom of the loaf in the center.

COOL ON A COOLING RACK. Repeat the baking process with the second loaf after allowing the oven and baking stone to come back to temperature, about 15 minutes. If the loaf is going to be eaten within 3 days, it is best kept on your countertop, unwrapped. The natural protection of the crusty exterior will preserve the soft interior crumb. For longer storage, wrap the loaf and store in the freezer. When ready to enjoy, thaw at room temperature and reheat in a 400°F (205°C) oven for 3 to 5 minutes.

CIABATTINA

Makes 16 rolls

Ciabattina, or ciabatta rolls, are a favorite at bakery cafés for gourmet sandwiches. To make these rolls, you simply pat the dough out and cut it into 16 equal pieces. Proof the ciabattina on a floured couche. You will also need to sprinkle cornmeal on the wooden oven peel so that these will slide off more easily. With the biga made ahead of time, these are rolls you can make in just over 5 hours.

DOUGH

1 cup plus 1 tablespoon and 1 teaspoon (200 g) Biga (page 116)

3 cups plus 3 tablespoons and 1 teaspoon (440 g) bread flour, plus more for dusting

2 teaspoons (11 g) salt

⅓ teaspoon (1 g) instant yeast

1 ½ cups plus 1 tablespoon (375 ml) water, 78–82°F (26–28°C)

Olive oil, for greasing

Cornmeal, for dusting

MIX THE DOUGH. To mix by hand, place the biga, flour, salt, yeast, and water in a bowl and mix with your hands or a dough scraper until you have a smooth and soft dough. Using a plastic scraper, turn the dough out onto a floured surface. Squeeze the dough through your fingers until the dough is so firm that you can't squeeze it through your fingers anymore, about 5 minutes. Continue to work the dough by stretching the dough horizontally with your fingers and hands. Then fold each side into the center, one over another, to form a long rectangle about 5 by 15 inches (13 by 38 cm), like a three-panel brochure. Repeat, dusting with a little flour as necessary, until the dough is smooth and elastic, approximately 5 times.

To mix using a stand mixer, place the starter, flour, salt, yeast, and water in the bowl of a stand mixer fitted with a dough hook. Mix for 5 minutes on low speed (the 2 to 3 settings on a KitchenAid), and then continue mixing for 5 minutes longer on medium speed (the 4 to 6 settings on a KitchenAid), or until the dough is smooth and elastic.

FIRST FERMENTATION. Transfer the dough to a stainless-steel bowl lightly greased with olive oil. Cover with a kitchen towel or plastic wrap and let rest for 3 hours at room temperature, above 72°F (22°C).

SHAPE AND FINAL FERMENTATION. Transfer the dough to a floured surface. With the flat of your hand, press the dough into a square. Divide into 16 pieces with a metal dough scraper. Using your hands, transfer each piece to a floured couche. Keep the dough squares separated. Each square should be about 2 by 2 inches (5 by 5 cm). Cover with a floured kitchen towel and let rest for another 1 ½ hours at room temperature before the final forming.

To prepare the oven for rebar steam baking, place an oven rack on the lowest rung of the oven. Arrange 10 small rebar in a single row along the bottom of a broiler pan; place the broiler pan on the lower oven rack. Arrange the second oven rack just above the broiler pan. Place a baking stone on the second, higher oven rack. After you load the loaf, pour ½ cup (120 ml) room-temperature water into the prepared broiler pan. Be careful of the hot steam. Quickly close the oven door.

To prepare the oven for cloche baking, place 1 oven rack on the lower third of the oven. Place a baking stone on the oven rack. Remove the second oven rack. When placing loaf in the oven, quickly invert a stainless-steel bowl over the loaf, creating a loose seal with the baking stone and close the oven door. Remove the stainless-steel bowl after 10 minutes of baking to release the steam.

BAKE. After preparing the oven for either method of steam, preheat the oven to 450°F (232°C) for 3 hours. Lightly coat a wooden peel with cornmeal. Gently place 8 rolls on the prepared peel. Slide the rolls off the oven peel onto the baking stone in the oven. (If using the rebar method, pour water into the broiler pan. If using the cloche method, place a stainless-steel bowl over the rolls immediately after sliding the rolls into the oven and remove the bowl after 10 minutes, as described above.) Total bake time is about 20 minutes, or until the rolls have turned a golden brown and sound hollow when tapped on the bottom of a roll in the center.

COOL ON A COOLING RACK. Repeat the baking process with the remaining 8 rolls after allowing the oven and baking stone to come back to temperature, about 15 minutes. If the rolls are going to be eaten within 3 days, they are best kept on your countertop, unwrapped. The natural protection of the crusty exterior will preserve the soft interior crumb. For longer storage, wrap the rolls and store in the freezer. When ready to enjoy, thaw at room temperature and reheat in a 400°F (205°C) oven for 3 to 5 minutes.

CIABATTINA

ITALIAN BREAD

Makes 2 long loaves or batards

Made with more flour than ciabatta, and more substantial, this traditional bread is seen on family tables throughout Italy. Make 1 loaf as an accompaniment to your next Italian meal, and save the second for sandwiches the next day. It's great with a garlicky butter or to sop up that delicious homemade pasta sauce.

DOUGH

1 ⅔ cups plus 1 tablespoon (320 g) Biga (page 116)

2 ¾ cups plus 3 tablespoons (400 g) bread flour, plus more for dusting

2 teaspoons (11 g) salt

¾ teaspoon (2.2 g) instant yeast

1 ¼ cups (300 ml) water, 78–82°F (26–28°C)

1 tablespoon plus 2 teaspoons (25 ml) olive oil, plus more for greasing

Cornmeal, for dusting

MIX THE DOUGH. To mix by hand, place the biga, flour, salt, yeast, water, and olive oil in a bowl and mix with your hands or a dough scraper until you have a smooth and soft dough. Pick up the dough with both hands and turn the dough out onto a floured surface. Squeeze the dough through your fingers until the dough is so firm that you can't squeeze it through your fingers anymore, about 5 minutes. Continue to work the dough by stretching the dough horizontally with your fingers and hands. Then fold each side into the center, one over another, to form a long rectangle about 5 by 15 inches (13 by 38 cm), like a three-panel brochure. Repeat, dusting with a little flour as necessary, until the dough is smooth and elastic, approximately 5 times.

To mix using a stand mixer, place the starter, flour, salt, yeast, water, and olive oil in the bowl of a stand mixer fitted with a dough hook. Mix for 5 minutes on low speed (the 2 to 3 settings on a KitchenAid), scrape down the bowl and the dough hook, and continue mixing for 5 minutes longer on medium speed (the 4 to 6 settings on a KitchenAid), or until the dough is smooth and elastic.

FIRST FERMENTATION. Transfer the dough to a stainless-steel bowl lightly greased with olive oil. Cover with a kitchen towel or plastic wrap and let rest for 1 ½ hours at room temperature, above 72°F (22°C).

PRE-SHAPE AND REST TIME. Transfer the dough to a floured surface. With the flat of your hand, press the dough into a round. Divide in half with a dough scraper. Using your hands, gently pat and guide each half into an oblong shape. Place the pieces on a floured work surface, seam side down. Cover with a floured kitchen towel and let rest for another 15 minutes before the final forming.

FINAL FORMING. Dust your hands with flour. Use a dough scraper to lift the dough pieces off the floured surface to begin the final forming. Pat down in a long oval shape, with the long portion oriented vertically. Fold the top one-third of the dough toward you and pat down. Take the top 2 corners of the shape and bring them to the center of the dough. Pat out the air. Turn the dough 180 degrees, repeat by folding the top one-third of the dough toward you, and pat down. Take the top 2 corners of the shape and bring them into the center of

the dough. Pat out the air. Hold the dough with your fingers on the back side of the dough and push the dough against the work surface with your thumbs, creating a seam. Touch up the shape of the dough by gently rolling the oval until the desired shape is achieved. Each oblong shape should be about 4 by 12 inches (10 by 30.5 cm).

FINAL FERMENTATION. Dust the work surface with flour and place each formed batard, bottom side up, on the surface. Cover loosely with a kitchen towel and let proof for 1 ½ hours at room temperature, above 72°F (22°C).

To prepare the oven for rebar steam baking, place an oven rack on the lowest rung of the oven. Arrange 10 small rebar in a single row along the bottom of a broiler pan; place the broiler pan on the lower oven rack. Arrange the second oven rack just above the broiler pan. Place a baking stone on the second, higher oven rack. Preheat the oven to 450°F (232°C) for 3 hours. After you put the loaf in the oven, pour ½ cup (120 ml) room-temperature water into the prepared broiler pan. Be careful of the hot steam. Quickly close the oven door.

To prepare the oven for cloche baking, place 1 oven rack on the lower third of the oven. Place a baking stone on the oven rack. Remove the second oven rack. When placing the loaf in the oven, quickly invert

a stainless-steel bowl over the loaf, creating a loose seal with the baking stone, and close the oven door. Remove the bowl after 10 minutes of baking to release the steam.

BAKE. After preparing the oven for either method of steam, preheat the oven to 450°F (232°C) for 3 hours. Lightly coat a wooden peel with cornmeal. Gently place 1 loaf on the prepared peel. With a bread lame or razor blade slanted at a 45-degree angle, make a lengthwise slash across the top of each loaf. Slide the loaf off the oven peel onto the baking stone in the oven. (If using the rebar method, pour water into the broiler pan. If using the cloche method, place a stainless-steel bowl over the loaf immediately after sliding the loaf into the oven and remove the bowl after 10 minutes, as described above.) Total loaf bake time is 30 to 35 minutes, until the loaf has turned a golden brown and sounds hollow when tapped on the bottom of the loaf in the center.

COOL ON A COOLING RACK. Repeat the baking process with the second loaf after allowing the oven and baking stone to come back to temperature, about 15 minutes. If the loaf is going to be eaten within 3 days, it is best kept on your countertop, unwrapped. The natural protection of the crusty exterior will preserve the soft interior crumb. For longer storage, wrap the loaf and store in the freezer. When ready to enjoy, thaw at room temperature and reheat in a 400°F (205°C) oven for 3 to 5 minutes.

SEMOLINA BREAD

Makes 2 round loaves or boules

This classic loaf is studded with sesame seeds on the outside. The recipe uses both bread flour and semolina. Semolina flour is ground from durum wheat, a hard spring wheat that is also used to make pasta. You can find it at better grocery stores or online from various millers (see page 21). The mix of flours yields a workable dough with a rich, nutty flavor and a wonderfully chewy texture.

DOUGH

¾ cup plus 1 tablespoon and 2 teaspoons (160 g) Biga (page 116)

2 cups (325 g) semolina flour

1 ¼ cups plus 1 tablespoon (180 g) bread flour, plus more for dusting

2 teaspoons (11 g) salt

⅔ teaspoon (2 g) instant yeast

1 ⅓ cups plus 2 tablespoons (350 ml) water, 78–82° F (26–28°C)

Olive oil, for greasing

Cornmeal, for dusting

TOPPING

⅓ cup (45 g) sesame seeds

MIX THE DOUGH. To mix by hand, place the biga, flours, salt, yeast, and water in a bowl and mix with your hands or a dough scraper until you have a smooth and soft dough. Pick up the dough with both hands and turn the dough out onto a floured surface. Squeeze the dough through your fingers until the dough is so firm that you can't squeeze it through your fingers anymore, about 5 minutes. Continue to work the dough by stretching the dough horizontally with your fingers and hands. Then fold each side into the center, one over another, to form a long rectangle about 5 by 15 inches (13 by 38 cm), like a three-panel brochure. Repeat, dusting with a little flour as necessary, until the dough is smooth and elastic, approximately 5 minutes.

To mix using a stand mixer, place the starter, flours, salt, yeast, and water in the bowl of a stand mixer fitted with a dough hook. Mix for 5 minutes on low speed (the 2 to 3 settings on a KitchenAid), scrape down the bowl and the dough hook, and continue mixing for 5 minutes longer on medium speed (the 4 to 6 settings on a KitchenAid), or until the dough is smooth and elastic.

FIRST FERMENTATION. Transfer the dough to a stainless-steel bowl lightly greased with olive oil. Cover with a kitchen towel or plastic wrap and let rest for 1 ½ hours at room temperature, above 72°F (22°C).

PRE-SHAPE AND REST TIME. Transfer the dough to a floured surface. With the flat of your hand, press the dough into a round. Divide in half with a dough scraper. Using your hands, gently pat or guide each half into a round shape about 6 inches (15 cm) in diameter. Let rest for another 15 minutes before the final forming.

FINAL FORMING. Dust your hands with flour. Use a dough scraper to lift the dough rounds off the floured surface to make sure they're not sticky. (If they are, gently brush your floured hands over the sticky places.) With your hands, pick up an edge of the dough and pull it to the center of the dough round. Make a quarter turn, fold the next edge to the center, and repeat this flattening, quarter turn, and repeat again. Then flip the dough over so the seams are facing down on the work surface. Cupping your hands, gently round the dough with pressure against the work surface. Repeat with the second dough round. Each boule should be about 6 inches (15 cm) in diameter.

FINAL FERMENTATION. Place the formed boules on a cornmeal-covered surface. Cover each boule loosely with plastic wrap or a kitchen towel and let proof for 1 ½ hours at room temperature, above 72°F (22°C).

To prepare the oven for rebar steam baking, place an oven rack on the lowest rung of the oven. Arrange 10 small rebar in a single row along the bottom of a broiler pan; place the broiler pan on the lower oven rack. Arrange the second oven rack just above the broiler pan. Place a baking stone on the second, higher oven rack. After you put the loaf in the oven, pour ½ cup (120 ml) room-temperature water into the prepared broiler pan. Be careful of the hot steam. Quickly close the oven door.

To prepare the oven for cloche baking, place 1 oven rack on the lower third of the oven. Place a baking stone on the oven rack. Remove the second oven rack. When placing the boule in the oven, quickly invert a stainless-steel bowl over the loaf, creating a loose seal with the baking stone, and close the oven door. Remove the bowl after 10 minutes of baking to release the steam.

BAKE. After preparing the oven for either method of steam, preheat the oven to 450°F (232°C) for 3 hours. Lightly coat a wooden peel with cornmeal. Gently place 1 boule on the prepared peel. With a bread lame or razor blade slanted at a 45-degree angle, make 3 horizontal and 3 vertical slashes (like a tic-tac-toe game), ⅛ to ¼ inch (3 to 6 mm) deep, across the top of each boule. Slide the boule off the oven peel onto the baking stone in the oven. (If using the rebar method, pour water into the broiler pan. If using the cloche method, place a stainless-steel bowl over the boule immediately after sliding the boule into the oven and remove the bowl after 10 minutes, as described above.) Total loaf bake time is 30 to 35 minutes, until the boule has turned a golden brown and sounds hollow when tapped on the bottom of the loaf in the center.

COOL ON A COOLING RACK. Repeat the baking process with the second loaf after allowing the oven and baking stone to come back to temperature, about 15 minutes. If the loaf is going to be eaten within 3 days, it is best kept on your countertop, unwrapped. The natural protection of the crusty exterior will preserve the soft interior crumb. For longer storage, wrap the loaf and store in the freezer. When ready to enjoy, thaw at room temperature and reheat in a 400°F (205°C) oven for 3 to 5 minutes.

FOCACCIA
WITH ROSEMARY AND THYME

Makes 1 (9 by 13-inch, or 23 by 33-cm) flatbread

Using the biga and a variety of flours in this classic Italian flatbread results in a spongy, airy crumb with a well-developed flavor, made even more delicious with the final slurry of olive oil and salt. Once you have made this, create your own signature toppings with sliced kalamata olives and strands of roasted red pepper, freshly grated Parmesan, or paper-thin slices of potato or tomato with an extra drizzle of olive oil. This flatbread bakes in a greased 9 by 13-inch (23 by 33-cm) baking pan, so the cloche baking method is not possible, as the pan will not accommodate the bowl. With the variation on this method, using steam for this recipe is optional. It is an enhancement, but focaccia is delicious without it. If you would like to use steam, the rebar method is your only choice.

DOUGH

⅓ cup plus 2 tablespoons (85 g) Biga (page 116)

2 ½ cups plus 2 tablespoons and 1 teaspoon (360 g) bread flour, plus more for dusting

2 teaspoons (5 g) rye flour

2 teaspoons (11 g) salt

¾ teaspoon (2.2 g) instant yeast

1 ¼ cups (300 ml) water, 78–82°F (26–28°C)

1 tablespoon (15 ml) olive oil, plus more for greasing

1 ¼ teaspoons (1.5 g) fresh rosemary leaves

Pinch of fresh thyme leaves

TOPPING

2 tablespoons (30 ml) olive oil

1 ½ teaspoons (8 g) salt

1 tablespoon (4 g) fresh rosemary leaves

MIX THE DOUGH. To mix by hand, place the biga, flours, salt, yeast, water, olive oil, rosemary, and thyme in a bowl and mix with your hands until you have a smooth and soft dough. Pick up the dough and turn the dough out onto a floured surface. Squeeze the dough through your fingers until the dough is so firm that you can't squeeze it through your fingers anymore, about 5 minutes. Continue to work the dough by stretching the dough horizontally with your fingers and hands. Then fold each side into the center, one over another, to form a long rectangle about 5 by 15 inches (13 by 38 cm), like a three-panel brochure. Repeat, dusting with a little flour as necessary, until the dough is smooth and elastic, approximately 5 minutes.

To mix using a stand mixer, place the starter, flours, salt, yeast, water, olive oil, rosemary, and thyme in the bowl of a stand mixer fitted with a dough hook.

Mix for 5 minutes on low speed (the 2 to 3 settings on a KitchenAid), scrape down the bowl and the dough hook, and continue mixing for 5 minutes longer on medium speed (the 4 to 6 settings on a KitchenAid), or until the dough is smooth and elastic.

FIRST FERMENTATION. Transfer the dough to a stainless-steel bowl lightly greased with olive oil. Cover with a kitchen towel or plastic wrap and let rest for 1 ½ hours at room temperature, above 72°F (22°C).

SHAPE AND FINAL FERMENTATION. Grease a 9 by 13-inch (23 by 33-cm) pan with olive oil. Transfer the dough to a floured surface. With the flat of your hand, press the dough into a square. Using your hands, gently pat and guide the dough into a long rectangle about the size of the pan. Transfer the rectangle to the prepared pan and press it so that it fully fills the pan. The dough should be an even ½ inch (1 cm) thick. Cover with a floured kitchen towel and let rest for another 60 minutes.

To prepare the oven for rebar steam baking (optional), place an oven rack on the lowest rung of the oven. Arrange 10 small rebar in a single row along the bottom of a broiler pan; place the broiler pan on the lower oven rack. Arrange the second oven rack just above the broiler pan. Place a baking stone on the second, higher oven rack. After you put the pan in the oven, pour ½ cup (120 ml) room-temperature water into the prepared broiler pan. Be careful of the hot steam. Quickly close the oven door.

BAKE. After preparing the oven for rebar (optional), preheat the oven to 450°F (232°C) for 3 hours. Immediately before putting the loaf in the oven, dimple the dough with your fingertips.

(Continued on page 134)

Drizzle olive oil over the top, sprinkle on the salt, and spread the rosemary evenly over the top. Slide the pan into the hot oven. If using steam, pour water into the broiler pan. Total bake time is 30 to 35 minutes, until the focaccia has turned a golden brown.

COOL ON A COOLING RACK. If the loaf is going to be eaten within 2 days, it is best kept on your countertop, unwrapped. The natural protection of the crusty exterior will preserve the soft interior crumb. For longer storage, wrap the loaf and store in the freezer. When ready to enjoy, thaw at room temperature and reheat in a 400°F (205°C) oven for 3 to 5 minutes.

BRAIDED CHALLAH

Makes 2 braided loaves

Adding biga to the classic sweetened egg bread makes the result even more voluptuous. If you like, you can make egg buns with this recipe, which are great for hamburgers and other sandwiches. But challah is so delicious just as it is. To get the dark, shiny finish, we brush the dough with beaten egg, known as an egg wash, before baking. Because of the egg wash, you will bake this on parchment paper on the baking stone. The paper will get a little scorched around the edges but will protect the stone from egg drips.

DOUGH

1 cup plus 1 tablespoon and 1 teaspoon (200 g) Biga (page 116)

2 ½ cups plus 1 tablespoon (350 g) bread flour, plus more for dusting

⅓ cup plus 1 tablespoon and 1 teaspoon (85 g) granulated sugar

2 teaspoons (11 g) salt

1 tablespoon plus ¼ teaspoon (10 g) instant yeast

¼ cup plus 2 teaspoons (70 ml) olive oil, plus more for greasing

¾ cup (180 ml) water, 78–82°F (26–28°C)

EGG WASH

2 eggs

MIX THE DOUGH. To mix by hand, combine the biga, flour, sugar, salt, yeast, oil, and water in a bowl and mix with your hands and a dough scraper until you have a smooth and soft dough. Squeeze the dough through your fingers until the dough is so firm that you can't squeeze it through your fingers anymore, about 5 minutes. Pick up the dough with both hands and turn the dough out onto a floured surface. Continue to work the dough by stretching the dough horizontally with your fingers and hands. Then fold each side into the center, one over another, to form a long rectangle about 5 by 15 inches (13 by 38 cm), like a three-panel brochure. Repeat, dusting with a little flour as necessary, until the dough is smooth and elastic, approximately 5 times.

To mix using a stand mixer, combine the biga, flour, sugar, salt, yeast, oil, and water in the bowl of a stand mixer fitted with a dough hook. Mix for 5 minutes on low speed (the 2 to 3 settings on a KitchenAid), scrape down the bowl and the dough hook, and continue mixing for 5 minutes longer on medium speed (the 4 to 6 settings on a KitchenAid), or until the dough is smooth and elastic.

FIRST FERMENTATION. Transfer the dough to a stainless-steel bowl lightly greased with olive oil. Cover with a kitchen towel or plastic wrap and let rest for 1 ½ hours at room temperature, above 72°F (22°C).

PRE-SHAPE AND REST TIME. Transfer the dough to a floured surface. With the flat of your hand, press the dough into a square. Divide into 4 even pieces with a dough scraper. Using your hands, gently form each piece into an 12-inch (30 cm) rope. Cover with a kitchen towel and let rest for another 15 minutes before the final forming.

FINAL FORMING. Dust your hands with flour. Roll each pre-shaped piece into a rope 24 inches (60 cm) long. For each 4-braid loaf, place 1 rope lengthwise left to right on a floured surface. Place the second rope over the first, forming a cross at a 90-degree angle. Braid by taking the top rope down, and bringing the bottom rope over and to the left of the top rope. Then bring the left rope right and over the right rope to the left. Continue this process until you have a braided loaf. Tuck the ends under to form a uniformly braided loaf. Repeat with the last 2 pieces of dough to make the second loaf.

(Continued on page 138)

1.

4.

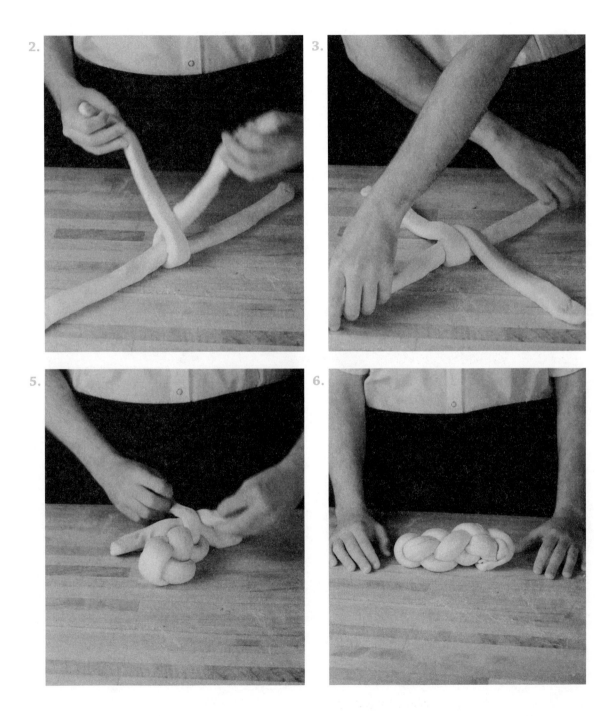

To prepare the oven, place 1 oven rack in the middle of the oven. Place a baking stone on the oven rack. Preheat the oven to 375°F (190°C) for 2 hours. (Challah does not require steam.)

BAKE. Line a wooden peel with parchment paper. Make the egg wash by whisking the eggs until smooth. Using a pastry brush, gently coat the braided loaves with the egg wash. Place 1 braided loaf on the wooden peel. Slide the loaf and parchment paper off onto the baking stone in the oven. Bake for 30 to 35 minutes, until the loaf has risen, turned a golden brown, and sounds hollow when tapped on the bottom of the loaf in the center.

COOL ON A COOLING RACK. Repeat the baking process with the second loaf after allowing the oven and baking stone to come back to temperature, about 15 minutes. Once the bread is fully cooled to room temperature, you can bag or wrap in plastic. For longer storage, wrap the loaf and store in the freezer. When ready to enjoy, thaw at room temperature and reheat in a 400°F (205°C) oven for 3 to 5 minutes.

ACKNOWLEDGMENTS

There are many influential and talented people who come to mind when I look back on my journey as a baker. The following have taught and supported me in becoming a better baker:

Claudio Cantore, my friend and mentor, who shared his skills, knowledge, and expertise. Baking is not simple or easy. Through example, he taught me the value of dedication, attentiveness, and hard work.

Claudio is a third-generation Italian baker. The Cantore family has been in the baking business for over 100 years. In the late 1980s, the artisan bread movement began in the USA. There were few bakers who understood the natural leavening process of old, and many people trying to rediscover these methods turned to Claudio.

Fred Spompinato, my friend and cofounder of Farm to Market, who shared a dream of baking great bread for Kansas City. Grains Galore and Sunny Black and Brown bread were Fred's creations. Fred infused into Farm to Market Bread the fact that "bread is part of modern man's search for authentic ways of being. It is something primal that can be experienced firsthand, something that is real and basic."

Kansas City, a great city and community that supports and takes pride in local business and local food. Thank you for your support!

INGREDIENT AND EQUIPMENT SOURCES

KING ARTHUR FLOUR

www.kingarthurflour.com
Customer Service 800.827.6836
King Arthur sells flour, grains, other ingredients, baking tools, and supplies.

BOB'S RED MILL

www.bobsredmill.com
Customer Service 800.349.2173
Bob's Red Mill sells flour, a wide range of grains, some tools, and supplies.

SAN FRANCISCO BAKING INSTITUTE

www.sfbi.com
Customer Service 650.589.5784
SFBI sells baking supplies: linen couche, wicker proofing baskets, oven peels, scrapers, and blades.

AMAZON

www.amazon.com
Customer Service 888.280.4331
Amazon sells baking stones and other baking supplies.

EPICUREAN

www.epicureancs.com
Customer Service 708.478.6032
Epicurean sells baking stones and other cutting surfaces.

PAMPERED CHEF

www.pamperedchef.com
Customer Service 888.687.2433
Pampered Chef sells baking stones and other baking supplies.

KITCHENAID

www.kitchenaid.com
Customer Service 800.541.6390
KitchenAid sells countertop appliances, electric mixers, cutting boards, and bakeware.

INDEX